D1399990

TWICE AS STRONG

12 SECONDS, 2 BROTHERS
AND THE MARATHON THAT CHANGED THEIR LIVES

JP & PAUL NORDEN

with DAVID SMITHERMAN

TWICE AS
STRONG

12 SECONDS, 2 BROTHERS,
AND THE MARATHON THAT CHANGED THEIR LIVES

JP & NORDEN
PAUL

With David Smitherman

© 2014 by Joseph Paul Norden and Paul Norden
All rights reserved. Printed in the United States of America. No part of this book may be used or reproduced in any manner without written permission except in the case of brief quotation for reviews.

For information, contact:
Palari Publishing
107 S. West St. PMB 778
Alexandria, VA 22314
www.PalariBooks.com
866-570-6724

Book website:
www.TwiceAsStrong.com

ISBN: 9781928662280, hardcover
Library of Congress Cataloging-in-Publication Data has been applied for.

First Edition

Co-writer: David Smitherman www.DaveSmitherman.com
Cover photos: Liz Cardoso, Global Click Photography
Cover design: Ted Randler
Photos: from the Norden family/friends private collections unless otherwise indicated
Editing: Kacy Drake

TABLE OF CONTENTS

strong
/strông/

adjective

1. solid, tough, not easily broken
2. able to withstand great force or pressure
3. not easy to break or damage

CHAPTER 1 – THE BARRICADE

For a split second, Jacqui Webb didn't understand why she was so high in the air. As a small woman, she's used to looking up at people and accustomed to making her way to the front of a crowd in order to see things that taller people likely take for granted. But for some reason, at this moment she could see farther than ever before. She watched as people scurried in every direction like startled deer leaping through a dewy meadow. Then she saw the smoke rolling quickly across the road, engulfing everything in its path. The strong odor of gunpowder assaulting her sense of smell.

Random images began tumbling around in her brain. Paul sitting beside her on a train. A lady selling flowers. A man with a small child. JP waving hello. Flat Stanley folded up in her purse.

Then she remembered the bone-shattering sound that had pierced the spring air only seconds ago. It had occurred only a few yards away. At first she wasn't sure if it was a firecracker or some other sort of celebratory craziness that sometimes happens at large events like this one that she and her friends often fill their weekends with, always cheering on the Red Sox at Fenway Park or checking out the special happenings for the Fourth of July... or attending the Boston Marathon. Boston is a large city known for its passionate residents, an exuberant display from the crowd is something to be expected. But this was somehow different.

To her, it looked like the building on the same side of the street was falling down as the mushroom cloud emanated out into the crowd, covering the spectators and athletes in a thick, choking dust. Soon, realization set in. She was standing on one of the metal barricades used to keep the crowds off the marathon course as the runners pant toward the finish line. She looked down below her and to see the Norden brothers supporting her, holding her up, pushing her toward the safe asphalt of Boylston Street.

After that first explosion, JP and Paul Norden looked at each other and both knew something sinister had just occurred. Being just over a year apart in age, the brothers have always hung out together, their instinctive ability to read each other is strong. JP realized what had happened wasn't good, but a bomb certainly was not his first thought. Maybe it was a gas explosion or some type of other malfunction in that building just a few yards away. It was difficult to discern. The crowd had gone from cheers and applause for the runners, to screams and cries. The noises, first the explosion and then the chaos from the crowd, made it hard to get a clear mental picture of what had occurred. But regardless of what it was, both men knew it was a bad sign. Each brother had arrived separately, each with a few friends in tow, but now they couldn't locate anyone. It was just the three of them in the middle of the madness—JP, Paul, and Jacqui—and the guys knew they had to first take care of her and then get the hell out of there.

Paul has never been particularly excited about huge events and large crowds. In fact, more often than not he would rather avoid them completely if at all possible. So a startling noise like the one he heard a few seconds ago was beyond nerve-wracking. It was the exact thing he always feared, something horrific happening to an unsuspecting and somewhat immobilized group of people. Anytime he made a decision to put himself in such a situation, it was for a very good reason. This time was no different. Mike Jefferson, a longtime buddy from the old neighborhood and friends with all of the Norden brothers, was running his first Boston Marathon in almost 10 years. This tight-knit group of friends from the small town of Stoneham always stick together and look out for each other. After finding out Mike was going to participate in the marathon, they pledged their support without hesitation. That's the way it's always been.

Less than a half mile away from the finish line, Mike was wearing headphones and carefully controlling his breathing. He focused on completing the marathon in under four hours, something he didn't think he could do that day. After checking his time at mile 22, he knew it wouldn't be a personal best, but running the treacherous course in under four hours might be a possibility. At that moment, he heard a loud noise up ahead. Unsure of what had happened, he pressed on, trying to keep focused on the task at hand. After coming over a bridge and seeing police officers blocking the course, he realized something was very wrong.

Mike quickly pulled off his headphones. "What's going on?"

"We've had a couple of explosions up ahead. Stay here," one of the officers replied forcefully.

Mike quickly reached for the small cellphone he had tucked in the rear waistband of his shorts, but found out all of the signals were jammed. No calls were going through. He wanted to check in with his friends and his family, including his mother, waiting for him at The Forum restaurant. Or maybe he could call his father. As a state trooper, he would certainly know what was causing this mayhem. Runners began to pile up as they came upon the impenetrable wall of police. This was not a good sign.

Soon, one of the officers came back with the news. "The marathon's over. No one past this point."

They wouldn't provide any more information, probably because no one knew exactly what was happening. Totally confused and concerned for his friends and family waiting up ahead, Mike started walking in the opposite direction while continuing to try his cell phone to no avail. He was not sure what to do next.

***

Sunday, April 14, 2013 was a typical spring day in Boston. It was sunny by lunchtime and there was a gentle, if slightly chilly, breeze. The next day, the day of the Boston Marathon, promised similar weather. JP and a friend met Mike at Felicia's of the North End, a favorite restaurant in Stoneham, to buy him lunch and wish him luck on the race. To their circle of pals, Felicia's is a place to hang out, see familiar faces, and take advantage of their huge portions, something Mike was particularly looking forward to on that day.

"I'm eating some pasta to get ready for tomorrow," Mike told them. "Gotta carb load for Marathon Monday," he said, still feeling the residual effects of a bit too much alcohol from the night before. There would be no drinking today, though. He was focused on tomorrow. After serving as a US Marine and now working as a firefighter, Mike knows when to let off a little steam or when to keep his head in the game.

The guys enjoyed hanging out and catching up and joking around.

"We're still planning to meet at The Forum on Boylston tomorrow, right?" asked JP.

"Yeah, that would be great," answered Mike. "A bunch of guys from work say that is a good place to hang out, party, and watch the runners since it is right at the finish line. I also told Paul, my mom, and some others to meet up there. Cool?"

"I never watched the marathon from there, but it's as good a place as any," replied JP as he finished his lunch.

***

Just a few miles away, Paul was at home making phone calls to see who else was going to meet up the next day. Mike had asked Paul if he would come hang out at the marathon. He and Paul have helped each other through plenty of tough times in the past, so Paul decided he would try to go because he wanted to show his support. Since crowded events like a marathon have a tendency to stir up his anxiety a bit, Paul felt better having other friends and family around. The bigger the group, the better. His girlfriend, Jacqui, was hard at work that day since the real estate market had picked up dramatically over the spring. While not back to pre-recession levels, sales were the strongest she had seen in years and she was making the most of it. While she was showing houses to perspective buyers, helping to make their family dreams come true, Paul continued his efforts to rally the gang for tomorrow.

Every year, the Boston Marathon is held on Patriot's Day, the third Monday of April. The marathon is one of the oldest and most famous in the world, dating back to 1897. With over a half-million onlookers and more than 20,000 participants, it is easily the most popular spectator sport in New England.

Patriot's Day is a state holiday which means schools and many offices across the state are closed. The city becomes practically immobilized with so many people packed along the 26-mile course of the marathon. The enthusiastic crowds are known for cheering on the runners, handing out water, and providing inspiration for them to finish the grueling trek. Traditionally, the celebrations begin at the 21 mile mark. Alcohol starts to flow as the racers make their way to the finish line on Boylston Street and are met by the awaiting parties at sidewalk restaurants and bars. To add to the festive atmosphere, the Boston Red Sox play a home game at Fenway Park which coincides with the marathon and serves to amp up the reverie, especially when the Red Sox are victorious.

On that Monday, Jacqui went to her office to finish up some paperwork before heading over to Paul's house to meet up for the marathon. She was dressed casually but prepared for the sometimes cool Boston spring weather with a gray T-shirt, black leggings, boots, and a denim jacket. Fortunately, the weekend had been quite successful as far as home sales go, but that meant it was slowing her down today of all days. She had to be at Paul's by 11:00 so they could make it downtown to meet the gang and see Mike cross the finish line. She knew how important it was to Paul, and she didn't want to miss it either. When she was finally done, she hopped into her car and made her way as quickly as possible, careful to avoid as much of the out-of-town traffic as possible.

Paul was waiting impatiently at his mother's house where he lived. As Jacqui came in, he was playing with the dogs that they both share—two Boxers, Bella and her pup, Baxtor.

"Sorry I'm late," Jacqui said as she bent down to pet the dogs.

Paul offered a lop-sided smile. Even if he was annoyed, he was always glad to see her. "No problem. I've been calling everyone and they all seem to be flaking out. At this point I don't even know who all is going."

"Should we take the dogs out?" she asked.

"No, I already did that. Let's just go," said Paul.

"Is anyone else here?

"Johnathan is asleep. Ma and Colleen went out shopping, I think."

"Don't you think you need a sweatshirt?" Before she had even arrived at the house, Jacqui knew he would be wearing his "uniform," as everyone called it—jeans, white T-shirt, Nike Air Max shoes, and his gray "B" fitted hat. To an outsider, with his multiple tattoos and smooth scalp, Paul can look like an intimidating tough guy, but his friends and family see beyond the exterior.

Exasperated, Paul sighed, "No, let's just go before we miss Mike's finish."

"I don't know what's up with everyone," she said. "I called a couple of friends that always go, but they were working today. Everyone is going to meet up at Angelo's later anyways so we'll see them one way or another. Where's JP?" Jacqui knew that Paul was a little anxious and having JP there would definitely make him feel better.

"Even he is going to be a little late," Paul added shaking his head. "His ride can't pick him up until around 1:00."

***

Earlier that morning, Mike had made his way to the marathon, which he hadn't run since 2004. He had been working out on the treadmill that January and became determined to take on the marathon that year. It was somewhat of a spontaneous New Year's goal that he had set for himself. So he called up his father to get assigned a number. Each year the local law enforcement is allotted a certain set of running spots to distribute, and with Mike being a veteran and firefighter, he agreed to give one to him.

Mike's mother had taken him to South Boston at around 7:00 a.m. to meet up with a bus that had been reserved to take the police officers and vets to the marathon in an effort to avoid parking hassles. After a mix-up with the numbers that morning, Mike found out that he was running under someone else's name. Once getting to the starting line, Mike waited for his 10:40 wave to be called. In the meantime, he saw his father zooming along the route on a motorcycle, escorting various vehicles into and out of the starting area. He waved his dad over for a quick chat before the run.

As his starting time got closer, Mike began to loosen up and prepare for the challenging 26-mile journey over hills, through tunnels, and eventually into the eager crowds being restrained by metal barricades along the streets of Boston. He was decked out in black running shorts, a Somerville Fire Department tank top that a friend had let him borrow, and a small cell phone tucked into the hidden back pocket of his shorts. Having not trained as much as he would have liked, Mike resigned himself to the fact that he wouldn't likely break the four-hour mark as he had in the past.

Completing the run in a decent time would be just fine this year. His wave was called and he was soon making his way across the challenging terrain, on his journey to the finish line where friends and family would already be celebrating.

***

When the two of them go out, Paul usually drives, but since her car was in the driveway and ready to go, Jacqui offered to take them to the train station where they planned to use mass transit and avoid parking obstacles in Boston. They were going to pick up one of Paul's friends, but asked him and anyone else who wanted to go to just meet up at the train station to save time. Originally, the plan was to gather at the Oak Grove station, but they changed it to the Malden Center to make things easier for everyone.

After parking in the garage, they headed up to the platform.

"Don't forget tomorrow is movie night," Jacqui said as she grabbed her purse from the car.

"Yeah, can't wait to see *42*. It looks really good," Paul smiled. "Let's get going. I'm freezing." They both love their Tuesday movie nights. It is their own little ritual. With Tuesday being bargain night, they save a few bucks and when a sports movie comes out, they are all over it.

"Ok, not to be a pain, but are you sure you don't want a sweatshirt?" Jacqui asked as she slipped on her jacket.

Starting to change his mind, Paul quickly dialed his friend to see if he could grab a jacket or something on his way.

"Dude, I'm almost at the station. Be there in five," his pal said.

As they got to the platform, Paul looked around. "Man, this has changed a lot since I used to take Colleen and Caitlin to Downtown Crossing for sneakers. Everything functioned with tokens and real people. It's all automated now."

"Well, that was a while ago," Jacqui noted. "Your sisters are all grown up now."

Since they are usually hanging out in and around Stoneham, Paul and his friends rarely take public transportation. Everything they need is just a few miles away. Going to downtown Boston is saved for big events or maybe a special night out, and even then traffic isn't usually too bad. Of course Patriot's Day is a different story entirely.

Being in the real estate business, it's Jacqui's job to be familiar with the area so while she doesn't use the train much, she does know a little about how it works, though even she was a bit out of touch with recent changes.

After punching a few buttons on the automated ticket machine, Paul got frustrated and Jacqui stepped in. "I think it's like $2 per person. Since there are a couple of friends coming, I'll get four tickets," she told Paul. He was just glad she was dealing with it. He didn't need any more stress.

"Hey, look, they are selling flowers. You want some?" Paul asked. He knew how much she loved small gestures like getting fresh flowers.

She smiled. "I do, but maybe when we come back. I don't want to have to carry them."

"You got it. I'll buy you some on the way home. That's a promise."

The couple milled around the station for a bit longer until they finally got a glimpse of one of their friends crossing the street. Jacqui rubbed Paul's arms and huddled in to keep him warm.

Thanks to all of the activities that day, the station was bustling. It was definitely busy for lunchtime on a Monday. There were all kinds of families and of course lots of Red Sox gear and even people carrying signs to wave at the marathon. Boston really knows how to turn it up when it's time for a celebration, that's for sure.

The group of friends, made up of a single guy and a newly joined couple, soon made their way up the platform. Everyone greeted each other and Paul breathed a sigh of relief. He had been waiting all morning and now they could get this show on the road.

"You guys, I only got enough tickets for four people and there are five of us. I wasn't sure who was going to show up," Jacqui told them.

"No worries," one of them said. "I have a CharlieCard that still has probably enough for one other person so we are good." He flashed the credit card-size electronic ticket that had taken the place of tokens several years ago. They all maneuvered through the electronic gate and Jacqui helped guide Paul because she knew he was out of his comfort zone. Soon the allotted money on the tickets she had bought ran out.

"Oh, I guess it is $2.50 instead of $2," Jacqui said.

"Good going," a friend joked predictably.

"At least I tried," she said.

They hurried back to the machine and added on a few more bucks to make sure everyone could make it on the train. Soon, the quintet was on the platform with Paul searching for a sliver of sunshine in an attempt to stay warm while they waited.

"It's OK," Paul assured them. "I'm fine."

Jacqui looked at him worried. "It's freezing if you ask me, but OK."

The gang talked about the week ahead. They are a tight group so when anyone makes plans, they don't hesitate to let everyone know. Everything is an open invitation in their circle of friends. The more the merrier is a way of life with the Stoneham-area locals. It's just always been that way.

They talked about bargain Tuesday at the movies and everyone agreed that *42* would be a can't-miss movie. Paul and Jacqui expected to get a couple of calls from friends who had decided to go or maybe just run into them at the theater tomorrow. Either way they hoped to see some familiar faces there.

On Wednesday, the girls already had plans to hang out together so Paul and the guys talked about possibly playing basketball. They are in several leagues with their pals and pickup games are common throughout the week. The conversation then turned to one of the guys and his new obsession.

"Didn't you start an Instagram account to display your paintings?" Jacqui asked him.

"Dude, what is up with those paintings?" his roommate asked. Since he and his girlfriend share an apartment with him, they had watched in amazement at his latest foray into the arts.

"I don't know why, but I like doing it," he said and for once he didn't seem to be joking.

Everyone laughed anyway.

Finally, the train arrived. The group watched as it eased in and came to a halt. It seemed unusually empty with so many people milling around, but that was likely because they were at the end—or the beginning—of the orange line. One of the train doors opened right in front of a still-shivering Paul. *That was lucky*, Jacqui thought to herself as she watched him stake out a spot in the warm train.

Jacqui slipped into the seat next to Paul while the couple grabbed the bench across from them. The single guy was happy to stand and hold on to the metal pole. Paul is slightly germ-phobic so it was amusing to watch him try to avoid touching anything on the bench.

"I think we are going to have to switch trains at Government Center," Jacqui informed the group.

"Let's just get there," their friend said. "I took off work for this, you know."

"What are you talking about?" Jacqui countered, "You work at a school. It's a holiday! Everything is closed!"

"No, I'm serious, you guys. I took off today to drink and tomorrow to recover!"

Everyone laughed at him, as usual.

Jacqui gave up making her point. As is often the case, she was not sure if he was kidding or not. It is hard to tell with him. Once he gets going, you never know what the guy will say. Jacqui was still convinced that he didn't take off time from work, but she didn't want to encourage him so she stayed quiet. Paul looked peacefully out the window as trees, houses, and buildings zoomed by.

The group disembarked from the train at Government Center and consulted the map to get their bearings. It was just as easy for them to drive into Boston on a regular day, so they were not familiar with which route to take to get to the location they had agreed upon for the marathon. They all decided that the green line should take them where they needed to go. And so they waited once again.

Being into fashion, Jacqui noticed her friend's top. "Is that shirt from Express?"

She smiled, "Yeah, I actually have it in every color. I love it."

"I almost wore that today, too. I worked there for five years!"

The train pulled into the station, and everyone made their way to the awaiting car. Once again, the train seemed usually empty, but that just meant they had more room to spread out and that Paul would be less anxious. It seemed like it would be a great day.

Just like before, one of them stood as Jacqui and Paul sat together and the lovey couple squished in tightly. They noticed an older man with a small child sitting across from them and everyone smiled at the boy's obvious excitement for the day's events.

As the men were chatting, Jacqui, always concerned about the details, texted a friend to ask which stop to get off at to be on the side of McGreevy's. That way they could make their way over to The Forum by being on the same side of the street. It was like putting together a puzzle. Crossing during the marathon was practically impossible, especially without a plan. And it seemed like no matter how many marathons they went to, the train system was always confusing on that day. While she waited for a return text, the group talked about which stops were open and which had been closed off because of all the happenings around town.

"Copley is closed today," said the man seated across from them.

"Oh, OK, thank you," Jacqui said. One the reasons they love

this city is because even the strangers are friendly. Everyone is so willing to help. It's comforting, especially when you are out of your element, like they were today.

As the group continued talking with their new friend about the challenges of taking the train only occasionally, Jacqui got her text. Her friend suggested getting off at Hynes Convention Center which would put them on Massachusetts Avenue. The text assured them that Mass Avenue was the best spot and they would be able to easily navigate their way to The Forum.

"That's where we should go," one of the guys said, "because Mike told me he would be meeting his family and a bunch of his firefighter buddies there after the run."

If you don't choose a location and let everyone know before time, it's almost impossible to arrange it in a crowd of that size. Paul and Jacqui knew where The Forum was located as they had been there a couple of years ago. Coincidentally, the occasion was a marathon fundraising party. So it was settled. The Stoneham group would all assemble at The Forum whenever they could and later that night they would celebrate at Angelo's.

Jacqui whispered to Paul. "I don't think Mass Ave. is the right stop. Sure it's the right side of the street, but with all of those cross streets it will be crazy."

"Let's just try it," Paul said.

The others chimed in their agreement.

***

It was getting late and JP was a little anxious himself, something the laid-back, affable guy rarely felt. His girlfriend, Kelly, couldn't hang out with the group because she had to work, so she had left a couple of hours ago. JP knew Paul and the others were meeting up early and, typically, he would have been right there with them. However, it just didn't work out today so he and his pals would be there a little later, but he was determined that they would arrive before Mike stepped across that finish line. JP wouldn't miss that for anything. Two of his buddies were already there. They were just waiting on one more to pick them all up—the one who was driving.

***

As the group on the train got closer to their stop, they watched as their car began to quickly fill to capacity. This was the crowd they had expected. It just seemed to take a little more time to fill up than they had originally thought. While that was fine for most, the girl traveling with them was escalating into a full-blown panic attack. People were squeezed into every square inch of the train so any type of personal space was nonexistent. At one of the stops, there were so many people pushing to get on that the train remained in the station, unable to close its doors. Despite the lack of room and instead of waiting for the next one, the determined crowd pushed in and the doors finally closed. Jacqui could understand why her girlfriend was responding in that way. It literally felt like there was no oxygen left; the sheer amount of people was overwhelming and something the group rarely experienced in their small town.

Jacqui tried to ease the tension by laughing it off and telling everyone to hang in there. It wouldn't be much longer now. Their single friend was standing beside the group and blocking one of the vacant seats. He could have just moved a bit to let someone sit down, but he was being difficult. He was always doing something unexpected like that.

A woman squeezed by the standing passengers and made her way past him.

"Can I have the seat?" she asked in a direct tone.

"I guess," he said, barely moving to allow her entrance.

She finally squeezed her way in, but just to make a point he continued standing way too close to her. Soon, the train came to a stop, and with a hiss that almost sounded like a gasp, the doors slid open. Once again, folks eager to make their way downtown tried to push into the overcapacity train car and again the doors had difficulty closing. Paul was starting to get a little antsy, but he calmed himself down, reminding himself that this was going to be a great day.

At the next stop, the woman sitting down asked the young man to move so she could get up. "Are you done saving space?" he asked her. "Are you done being an asshole? Oh, wait, you always were!" she replied and with that she stormed out of the car as the door shut behind her.

The group let out a little giggle, more for a release of tension than anything else, and their friend finally sat down after making his point—whatever that had been. This was not what they had expected when they had set out this morning, and their journey wasn't over yet. Thank goodness they would get off at the next stop. After they exited, they made their way through the thousands of people clogging the streets. The sheer density of the crowd was astounding to them. It was like being trapped in a life-size ant farm.

As they made their way to Boylston Street, the epicenter of

the final section of the marathon, they saw even more people, of all ages—families, couples, groups of children. It looked like a crowd scene from a movie, like a computer-generated mob. That many actual people in one place felt unimaginable.

The group of friends snaked their way through the crowd with the guys leading and the girls holding on tight to make sure they didn't get separated in this chaos. Just then Paul noticed something ahead.

"Look, a pretzel truck! I'm going to get a pretzel."

Jacqui just shook her head. She knows Paul is not a big foodie, but when he gets focused on something there is no stopping him. Currently, he was all about soft pretzels and they aren't so easy to find. So as far as he is concerned, everything else stops when he comes upon them. It's pretzel time. After he got two of them, they moved onward. As they passed a firehouse, they could see the barricades situated up ahead signaling that their path was blocked.

Jacqui's suspicions had been correct. The runners were being directed to turn from Hereford Street onto Boylston Street and then to the finish line. That meant their chosen route was blocked off.

Paul was happily polishing off his first pretzel as Jacqui yelled to him over the steady hum of the crowd. "Isn't it crazy in here?"

Paul looked a bit dazed by the sheer volume of people. Everyone knew that crowds and drinking were two things he was not fond of. An event filled with intoxicated spectators didn't sit well with him. However, he seemed to be handling things rather well under the circumstances.

Typically it was Jacqui, JP, and a couple of other local guys at events like this. They love the energy and excitement and it's a fun thing for them. So, as they always do in this group of friends, they don't hesitate to split into various formations based on what they like to do, knowing that at the end of the day, everyone usually meets up at the same place—often Angelo's—to hang out and share stories.

Jacqui remembered what it had been like a couple of years ago when she went. There had been six of them, and as it usually happens, they had also gotten off the train at the wrong stop, but that time they had decided to rent bicycles to get to their designated meeting area. It had been so hot and they had to ride two-by-two to get through the crowd, but it had worked. Jacqui thought maybe they could do that again this year as a way to get to The Forum faster. However, the riders they talked to said it would take a long time to get up there and, regardless, they would have to backtrack to get to the rental station.

The gang stopped to re-group and make some decisions. Should they just eat now and maybe it would be easier to get by later? Do they find a place to cross the street? Should they just keep going?

Paul, still chewing his last pretzel, suggested that they just press on. Jacqui took a couple of bites of the soft snack and agreed. They were able to make some headway down Dalton Street and once they turned the corner they saw a row of taxis. They were elated. They just hoped it wasn't a mirage. It seemed like the heavens were answering their prayers. It really was going to be a great day. The taxis were of particular relief to the ladies whose feet were already sore from their journey. A cab ride would be perfect right about now, especially since it also felt like it had gotten a little chillier.

Jacqui suggested that they buy a sweatshirt for Paul before

going farther, but he waved her off. They knew he never wanted to inconvenience anyone, but as far as they were concerned, it was no big deal to stop for a couple of minutes.

"Yeah, we can get you a nice Boston shirt, man," one of his friends yelled.

While he loves his hometown, Paul has always followed the Baltimore Ravens and Los Angeles Angels so he wasn't too thrilled with that idea. Paul rolled his eyes as the group made its way to the taxis stand just ahead. "Let's just go," he said.

***

JP was still waiting at his place a few miles from his mother's house. He had talked to Kelly on the phone to tell her they were about to leave and he would catch up with her after the marathon, once she was finished with babysitting. Unlike Paul, JP enjoyed going to big events and celebrating by having a few drinks with some buddies. He had been to the marathon plenty of times and it was always lots of fun, but now it was 1:00 and his ride was nowhere to be seen.

***

Jacqui quickly approached one of the awaiting taxis and asked, "Can you take us to Arlington Street?" That's where the bikers had directed them to go.

The cab driver nodded.

"Can you squeeze all five of us in there?"

He quickly shook his head no. That's OK. They would split up. Jacqui, Paul and their friend hopped into the first cab while the lovebirds got in the one directly behind them. As the first group arrived in front of the Niemen Marcus store, they called the others. "Our taxi driver can't make it up that way. He's taking us to the Fenway section. Call us later."

"You got it. Talk to you soon."

This meant the group was down to three and they were determined to see Mike finish the race. Then maybe they would meet up with the others or just hang out at The Forum. They were going to play it by ear. Jacqui sent a text to Mike's sister to make sure they were all still planning on meeting up later. She knew that plans could easily change and she wanted to double-check before they went ahead.

Once the meeting place was confirmed, they again set out on foot. They were walking much more than any of them had anticipated. They passed by runners, families gathered in groups, a section of buses, it seemed to go on forever, like one of those cartoon backgrounds that repeat on a loop. Finally, they came upon a police officer.

"Keep walking all the way down and you'll be able to cut across," he directed them.

After another 30 minutes, they were finally able to cross the road and soon they had found The Forum. At last!

***

At around 1:20, the driver finally arrived at JP's house to take the rowdy group into Boston and keep the party going. JP quickly called Paul.

"Where are you guys?"

"We're already at The Forum. A bunch of people are here," Paul said.

JP thought it was odd that they were meeting up on that side of the street because it was a lot more difficult to get over there, and they had never done it before. JP had not even been that close to the finish line because it was always the busiest area on the course. He thought about suggesting another place, but didn't want to mess up everyone's plans. He just wanted to get on the road to meet up with his brother and everyone else gathering there to cheer on Mike.

**

Jacqui remembered that she had her younger cousin's Flat Stanley with her. He had given her the character from the children's book so she could take pictures of him in unique locations as part of his school project. On Easter Sunday, she had decided to take Flat Stanley and show him what Boston was all about. The week before, she and Paul had taken a picture of him at a Celtics game and, now, she decided that the Boston Marathon was the perfect spot for yet another Flat Stanley photo op.

"Why don't you get a picture in front of the finish line?" Paul suggested. "You can show him with all of the international flags in the background."

Jacqui retrieved the character from her bag and had Paul take a few photos of the two of them. "Take one more," she said. "Just to make sure."

Paul rolled his eyes, but did as he was asked.

"Good!" she squealed. "I like that one." It didn't matter to her that it was going to a group of second-graders, Jacqui liked giving everything her best. She loved the fact that it had worked out that they were able to get this picture at the iconic finish line of this event. What a coup.

As the three of them stood at the finish line (four if you count Flat Stanley), they watched as runners completed the course, grabbed food and water, and covered themselves in plastic jackets to restore their body temperature. They examined the hundreds of flags attached to the metal barriers that represented nations from around the world supporting runners in the marathon.

After approving the photos, Jacqui carefully folded Stanley back up and placed him neatly in her Michael Kors crossover bag. Despite the fact that it was stuffed with necessities, Flat Stanley fit perfectly. She couldn't wait to show her cousin the photos they had taken. The trio of friends watched a few more runners cross the finish line and then they each checked their phone messages and took a few more photos as they waited for JP and the others to arrive.

***

At the 20-mile mark, Mike saw that he was under the three-hour time. Despite not training and Paul joking with him about how he might not even finish, it looked like he could actually complete the run in under four hours. Once he reached the 22-mile mark, Mike stopped for a bathroom break, excited that he might finish the race faster than anticipated, something he could brag about when everyone got together. He was definitely celebrating tonight. He quickly checked his phone before jumping back on the course. He hadn't looked at it since he had started running.

JP had sent a text that said *GOOD LUCK* at around 10:00 that morning. Just then the phone rang. It was from Paul.

"Paul? Hello?"

Silence. Mike couldn't hear anything but background noise.

"Yo, Paul?" There was no response. Maybe he was letting Mike know he was on the way or possibly he was already along the route and couldn't hear with the crowd. Hell, maybe it was an accidental pocket dial. Who knows? Paul was probably calling to give him some last-minute encouragement. Mike smiled and put the phone away. He knew he'd be seeing everyone soon enough.

***

JP and his friends finally made it to Boston and found parking in a relatively short time. They were surprised at how things had worked out. Naturally, they were disoriented like everyone else and had parked on the opposite side of the street. They began to make their way to the side where The Forum is located so that they could finally meet up with Paul and the others. A walk that would take five minutes on any other day ended up lasting almost an hour as they weaved back and forth through the crowd until finally crossing the busy road.

The foursome stayed focused and walked along Boylston Street, past the fire station, then they made their way to Newbury Street, over to Massachusetts Avenue, back down and then up. At one point, one of the guys needed a bathroom break and asked his friends to hang on. He ducked into a bar and seemed to be gone for a long time. There was probably a crazy huge line, but JP was getting antsy. This trip seemed almost like it was moving in slow motion. He just wanted to get there. He just wanted to find his brother, the rest of their friends, and have some fun.

***

Jacqui and Paul walked over to The Forum to see what was going on there while they waited for JP. The bouncers checked their ID's and the guys went in, leaving Jacqui to fish through her small bag to find her license. She gave the bouncer a slight smile when all she could find was Flat Stanley. He just glared at her. After the journey she had just made, she wasn't about to let some random bouncer kill her mood. The duo was greeted by the hostess who informed them that because of Patriot's Day there was a $25 cover charge. They were tired, thirsty, and hungry, but no one wanted to pay a cover, especially when they weren't even certain that everyone else was going to stay there.

Paul suggested that they might want to see if Mike's mother and their family were in there before they paid. As they stood in the doorway weighing their options, they turned around and Mike's mom was in front of them. Things were finally looking up. They told her they weren't excited about paying a cover and she agreed.

"Do we know how far away Mike is?" Jacqui asked her.

"I'm trying to track him on my cell phone, but I can't figure it out!"

One of their friends was nearby and overheard. "Give me his number and I'll track him for you guys."

They exchanged information since Mike's mother was aware of his runner number, despite the name mix-up that had occurred that morning. Jacqui talked to Mike's aunt because she knew the family since her sister had actually dated Mike. The small Stoneham area creates interpersonal relationships that sometimes make for slightly awkward situations, but for the most part everyone gets along. Now was no different.

"Mike's gotta be pretty close!" Someone shouted to the group.

After hearing that, Jacqui decided to see if she could snag a front row view, so she pulled herself along the barriers in an effort to relieve the pressure on her blistered feet. "Look at all the soldiers running in full gear!" she whispered to Paul.

"I know it's insane," he agreed. They watched for a moment in silence.

"It brings a tear to my eye when I see that," she said as he nodded. Paul remained close to Jacqui to make sure she didn't get lost and to help ease his anxiety as they waited for his brother.

"Oh, sorry guys," a friend yelled, "I might have read this wrong. He might not be as close as I thought."

It didn't really matter to the group. They were there for the immediate future anyway. They deserved a rest. While their travel friend was off socializing, Paul and Jacqui passed the time taking more photos, first of the runners approaching and then of their backs as they crossed the finish line victoriously, arms outstretched.

Paul checked his phone to see if JP had tried to contact him. It was so noisy that he wouldn't hear it if it rang. He noticed that he had accidentally called Mike. He thought about calling him back but didn't want to bother him. He was probably close to the finish line at this point. Just then his phone chirped. It was JP.

"We made it. We're in Boston. Where are ya?"

"We're at The Forum. Hurry up!"

"OK," JP said, "we'll be there soon. Don't move! One of the guys is holding us up. Damn pee break!"

Jacqui and Paul know JP is good with directions so he should be arriving in no time. They weren't sure how those guys had managed to drive into the city and park so quickly, but they were just glad he would be there soon.

After about an hour, JP finally arrived. Jacqui pointed him out to Paul and watched as his face lit up. They are brothers and fight like any other siblings, but it never lasts long. They are both sufficient on their own, though together it's almost like they can do anything. Their unspoken bond is obvious to everyone around them. Because they are so close in age, they share many of the same friends and often find themselves at the center of a group gathering, the nucleus around which the others rotate.

Paul's energy noticeably improved upon JP's arrival. The group was finally together and everyone could now focus on the marathon and cheering on Mike as he sailed across the finish line.

"Hey, so where's Mike?" JP asks. "Does anyone know yet?"

"They are trying to find him on the tracker, but not having much luck. Something about a different name. I don't really know," Paul said. "Should we just try and get something to eat now?"

"Lemme check with his mom first," JP said.

"I found him," someone said. "Definitely the 22-mile marker. Like 15 minutes away." It was about 2:30.

The group shifted their focus to the marathon course. JP and Paul were a few rows of people back, but Jacqui had wormed her way up to the front of the crowd. She held on to the barricade hoping to snap a picture of Mike as he ran by since the others might not be able to see very well. As she focused on the runners, examining each one to see if she could spot him, she heard people yelling and cheering on either side of her. The roar was overwhelming, but she was on a mission and she wasn't about to abandon it now! She watched as the exhausted runners headed for the finish line soaked in sweat, looking both miserable and relieved.

She watched as children hopped the barriers to meet their parents and run the last lap together. The girl next to her started banging passionately on a US Postal mailbox. The noise was almost unbearable. It seemed like it kept building, like it would never stop. Jacqui considered moving over because she had mailbox girl on one side and a lady screaming for every single runner on the other side. However, she had prime sidewalk real estate where she was and she did want to relinquish it. She wanted to get a good photo to show everyone later. It would just be a few more minutes anyway.

She turned to look behind her to get a visual on her group of friends, making sure to always keep them in eyesight so they didn't get separated. She waved at Paul and saw JP talking with a bunch of guys that had just arrived. Paul smiled at her and everything seemed a little easier. She turned her attention back to the runners as mailbox girl continued to kicked the metal, her rhythm seeming to pick up its pace.

Just as she looked down the street to see if she could locate Mike, a huge noise erupted, filling the air, the jolt almost knocking her down. Jacqui steeled herself against the barricade and watched as a huge cloud of smoke oozed its way across the street like some spontaneous, evil dust storm. Immediately, Jacqui knew something was not right.

Paul and JP looked at each other when the first explosion

cracked through the air. It was such a loud noise that they were both shaken by it. They felt the sidewalk vibrate first at their feet and then the sound waves traveled up their bodies. JP knew his brother was shifting into anxiety mode and rightly so.

Anxious as he was, Paul quickly looked over to see Jacqui trying to make her way to them. The crowd started to disperse, unsure of what was happening. The cheers were now screams and people were bumping and pushing each other.

One of the guys looked up from his iPhone and yelled as loud as he could, "That was a bomb! That was a bomb! That was a bomb!"

Another friend yelled, "Get into the street!" as he stood by the barricade, waving the others to come over.

"We gotta get into the road," JP instructed them.

Jacqui, Paul, and JP tried to push their way toward the open area of the street where there would be room to move. They could get away from the buildings and run in one direction or the other. It didn't matter where; they just knew they couldn't stay at that location. The metal barricades were an issue because they worked perfectly. They kept the crowd out of the street, but it was now imperative that they overcome those obstacles.

Paul and JP grabbed Jacqui on either side and lifted her small body into the air. She suddenly found herself balancing on the metal bar, and she knew what she had to do. She needed to get into the street quickly and then make sure the Nordens were behind her. No one was sure what else could happen. Were buildings falling? Was there a fire? Would there be a stampede? It was all so confusing.

As the Norden brothers held Jacqui, balancing her on the barrier, they looked at each other. It was obvious that this was not a good situation. They have been together through so many tough times that relying on each other is never a question. They were going to get Jacqui to safety and then hop over this friggin' barrier and the three of them would be just fine. They had to be.

They both looked up to see if she was ready to jump when they saw her looking down the street at the smoke and pandemonium. At that moment they felt her get yanked from their grip as the second, stronger explosion erupted directly behind them. Paul tried to grab her as Jacqui was blown off the barricade and through the air. In an instant, the brothers were pummeled into the metal barriers, their bodies bouncing along the sidewalk as Jacqui was tossed onto the asphalt.

CHAPTER 2 – TWELVE SECONDS

For just a few brief moments, as the earth-shattering explosion began to loosen its chokehold on the unsuspecting crowd, an eerie calm fell over the startled spectators near The Forum Restaurant on Boylston Street. It was as if no one was sure what had just happened. What bizarre event had crashed into their lives on this fun-loving Boston afternoon?

There had been twelve seconds between the two explosions. JP and Paul had taken the brunt of the second blast, shielding those in front of them as Jacqui sailed through the air. Just as they had been hoisting Jacqui over the barricade and into the perceived safety of the street, they felt the rush of the second boom pummel their legs and back, dagger-like pain shooting throughout their bodies. As they were pounded to the sidewalk by the sheer impact, Jacqui was hurled into the street while the crowd screamed and ran in all directions, their natural flight instinct taking hold.

After the first explosion, JP saw some people crying, some clapping, some screaming—no one seemed sure how to respond, the shock of the intrusion overwhelming them. JP knew this shouldn't be happening. He quickly did a mental checklist—no way was this a celebratory cannon or some type of military salute, but it possibly could have been a gas explosion, maybe coming from one of the manhole covers. But after that first boom, he saw actual flames and that's when he and Paul went into protection mode.

Once the second, unavoidable blast assaulted them, JP found himself rolling around on the sidewalk in intense pain. It was such an immediate stabbing sensation that he thought he may have gotten punched—*some drunk bastid gettin' crazy on marathon day*—it happens. But as he further assessed his situation, he could see that his pants were actually on fire. *Holy shit! This is bad.* As he tried to rise up and deal with the flames, he felt himself fall down again and he realized that he couldn't support his weight. Something didn't feel right. That's when he saw that his right leg was mangled, and part of it was missing. Below his knee it was blank, empty, like it had been erased. He had tried to stand up with only a stump where his leg used to be.

Oh, shit, this is real bad, he thought, but, somehow, he stayed focused. *I gotta see what else I'm dealing with.* While his left leg was still attached, it was gaping open, exposing flesh, blood, and bone. Not only that, his pants were still on fire, scorching his skin. As he slapped the flames and tried to roll his body against the ground, he could feel the sensation of heat on his back. He knew he was burned very badly. Then as the smoke cleared, he scanned the chaotic crowd to find his brother.

Only about six feet away, Paul was sitting up and staring into the street at his right leg. Oddly enough, it was not attached to him but laying on the asphalt, floating untethered amidst the stampeding crowd. He had the urge to reach for it, grab it. After all it's part of him. Maybe he could save it. Then he remembered that he needed to find his brother and his girlfriend. They had to be nearby. He wiped away some of the blood and soot from his eyes and scanned the crowd. He couldn't focus, couldn't make out anyone that he knew. It was like he had been dropped in a foreign place. Nothing looked familiar.

JP saw Paul sitting up, looking dazed. He searched the ground and realized Paul's leg was missing as well as his own. He yelled to Paul, trying to get his attention through the cacophony of screams. It seemed like a dream. It was difficult to comprehend that seconds ago they have been laughing, joking around, and goofing off. Now they were both mounds of flesh on the sidewalk, limbs detached from their bodies, burns covering their skin, hot shrapnel burrowed into them. Being the older brother, JP always feels instinctively protective, not that Paul needs it of course, but it is a natural response. They grew up together, worked in the roofing business together, and even despite JP living on his own, they see each other almost every day.

Now the physical distance between them seemed to have grown, stretching out for miles. During tough times, they had been raised to help each other when the chips were down, but Paul couldn't hear JP yelling for him. There was too much going on, and the blast had lacerated their eardrums, damage that would never fully mend. It was frustrating for them both. JP could see Paul, but couldn't hear him. Paul had looked for JP, but wasn't able to find the familiar, jovial face in the crowd. They had to get out of this. They had to make sure the other was OK.

In addition to his physical disfigurements, Paul was coherent enough to be concerned about his mental state. He was always aware of his propensity for anxiety and panic attacks, something that could hamper his all-important decision making skills now. Not being able to locate JP or Jacqui didn't help, but he knew he had to push through it. He had to keep a clear head. He also somehow needed to let Ma know what happened.

A stranger ran up to him and identified himself as former military, probably to instill confidence in Paul that he knew what he was doing. "Am I going to die?" Paul asked directly. He's never one to beat around the bush. He'd rather have the facts and deal with them head on. "I feel like I'm going to have a panic attack," he gasped.

"It's OK," the comforting voice assured him. "We are going to get help. Don't worry."

Soon he was flanked by several others who wasted no time in applying a crude makeshift tourniquet to his leg and making a valiant attempt to address his most serious wounds. He couldn't focus on their faces, it was such a blur of bodies and hands covering him with their shirts and belts—anything they could find to stop the bleeding. Finally Paul saw the familiar blue uniforms of two first responders who immediately eased him onto a backboard in preparation for an ambulance that would hopefully arrive soon.

JP felt a bit of relief as he saw Paul being hauled away, it even looked like he was talking on his cell phone. That gave JP time to focus on his own injuries. It seemed like a long time before anyone came over to him, but in actuality it was only a few seconds. A similar scene played out for him—guys doffed their shirts and belts for tourniquets and crude bandages. "I'm feeling really dizzy," JP said, not sure how loud he was speaking. "You are going to be all right," someone told him. "Just lie down here. More help is coming." JP felt a little better with that reassurance. He thought maybe he could hear an ambulance siren, but since everything sounded muffled and tinny he wasn't sure.

Dazed and in shock, Jacqui found herself sitting in the street, the same street she had seen in front of her as she stood on that barricade just seconds before. She distinctly remembered looking down Boylston Street after the first explosion and seeing the eerie remnants of a charred building along with a huge mushroom cloud. It reminded her of the horrific scene at the World Trade Center over a decade ago. She had the odd sensation that there would be multiple explosions working their way up toward the group so when someone yelled to get into the street, she wasted no time in doing just that. She had felt herself rising in the air and realized Paul and JP were helping her over the metal railing that blocked their path. Then everything went black.

When she regained her senses, she realized she was in the street surrounded by the pungent smell of sulfur. She could feel her skin burning all over, soot covering her face. Jacqui slowly stood up, trying to figure out what had happened. She couldn't make out anything through the thick smoke that choked her throat and burned her eyes. There was a loud, constant ringing in her ears. She tried to make out the sounds around her, but everything was muffled, like she was underwater.

Just then she felt an intense burning sensation on her hand and realized her rings were searing her fingers. She instinctively grabbed at them, twisting and turning them in a desperate attempt to free herself from the hot metals. At first they wouldn't budge, but she was focused and soon she felt them loosen and slip off. She quickly hurled them into the street and yelled at an approaching police officer.

"I need help," she tried to say. With her impaired hearing, she wasn't sure if he could hear her since she couldn't hear herself. All she heard was that damn ringing sound. It briefly flashed her back to the scene just before the blast with the banging mailbox and the exuberant screams.

The policeman put his arm around her and guided her to the curb. Just then another man came toward them on Boylston. "I'm an off-duty firefighter," Jacqui heard him say. Suddenly she got a burst of energy. She could hear! She actually heard him speak! She felt relieved until he said, "We have to be careful. I don't know if there were chemicals in that bomb."

Oh, hell no, Jacqui thought, as she instinctively shed what was left of her clothes to show that there was no other danger. "I need help...now!" she yelled. The firefighter quickly pulled off his sweatshirt and slipped it over her. Several other people passed by and each handed over another article of clothing. In her mismatched outfit, Jacqui finally sat down to assess the situation. *I've got to think this through.* Just then she looked down and saw her leg. A huge wound traveled along the femur, exposing so much bone and blood that she realized if she was going to keep her wits about her, she had to steel herself. *Just don't look at it*, she thought. *Just don't look.*

Her hands were bleeding profusely, she had never seen blood oozing out of her body so quickly. She felt a little dizzy and her hearing seemed to be going in and out. The sounds around her ebbed and flowed with oceanic repetition. It was difficult to distinguish who was talking with her hearing still going in and out. It was hard to identify the sounds around her. She looked down and saw tissue, skin, and blood littering the ground below.

Facing the origin of the explosion, she frantically searched the scene across the street. The oppressive smoke had lifted and she saw JP sitting up, looking dazed, surrounded by twisted metal from the barricades; the mailbox she had been standing beside was blackened with smoke rising off of it. Several people were around JP and they were adjusting him in a flurry of hands and makeshift bandages. She craned her neck to see past them, to get a better glimpse of her friend. Soon there was an opening in the crowd and she got a good look. JP's face was covered in soot, bandages wrapped around him, and as she looked down she saw that that his leg just stopped at a bandage. It just wasn't there.

During this time, people were grabbing tablecloths and other material from nearby restaurants and someone threw one over Jacqui to keep her protected. "Am I losing my leg?" she asked anyone who would answer as she watched JP struggle. Then she noticed a woman in front of her, in the middle of the street, also without one of her legs. It was unbelievable to watch the mayhem unfold. It seemed like some kind of dream or a bad horror movie. How could this be happening at the marathon?

As she continued surveying the scene, she finally located Paul. He was just a few feet from JP but facing the other direction. He was sitting up and it looked like he was talking to the people surrounding him. Jacqui pointed at him and yelled to the firefighter, "You need to tell him that I'm OK. He needs to know I'm OK. He's my boyfriend. He will be worried."

"Which one?" the guy asked.

"The one sitting up," she said adamantly. It was so crowded and chaotic, the man had no idea who she was talking about, but to her it was clear. He was right there. She could see him. And it looked like he was not as badly injured as JP, but if that was the case, why wasn't he getting up? He seemed more coherent somehow and that had to be a good sign. She was so glad she could see him, but felt so disconnected from him. He was just across the street, but so far away.

After she saw Paul lying down on a board, she took stock of the scene around her. It was sheer and utter chaos as people ran back and forth across the street, some getting as far away as possible and others trying to assist the wounded bodies that littered the asphalt. The smoke had completely cleared now and it was obvious that many people were injured, and most looked very serious. She could tell that the majority of the spectators had cleared out, but she was amazed that so many people stayed to help. It was obvious that their assistance was crucial in administering critical care quickly.

Then Jacqui realized her stomach and her back had burns on them and her skin felt so hot she could barely tolerate it. She started yanking off the tablecloths and donated clothes, but was told repeatedly to keep them on to protect her. "My skin is burning! It hurts."

"Just keep them on," she was told. "We're getting help."

Then a woman ran up to her. "I'm a doctor. Do you need help?"

"Yes, please, can you look at my leg?"

"Well, I'm an anesthesiologist. Not sure if I can help with that."

"Can you call my mom?" The woman pulled out her phone, but the situation was obviously affecting her as well. Jacqui saw her hands shaking as she waiting for Jacqui to give her the numbers to dial. It took Jacqui a minute to think. *Slow down and concentrate*, she thought. *You know this*. And just as she did, it came to her. The woman dialed the phone. No answer. "OK, here is my sister's number," Jacqui said, not giving up. The woman dialed again and this time began leaving a message. Jacqui thought the woman was talking to her sister. "Let me talk to her!" As the phone was put to her ear she yelled, "I've been hurt. There was an explosion. I—" Then she realized it was voicemail. There was no one on the other end. "Here's my aunt's number." Again, no answer.

Jacqui felt a bit defeated. Her own phone and all of her belongings had been blown away from her during the blast. She needed to connect to someone. She looked up at the woman to get her to re-dial everyone again and realized that she was gone. Just then another guy came up to her.

"I'm going to wrap up your leg real quick. We have several people who lost limbs and we have to take them first, but we will be back for you. Just wait here and stay calm. Don't worry."

She just looked at him bewildered as she held the gauze in place and watched him dash off to help someone else. Another man approached and Jacqui immediately asked him to give her mom a call. This time she answered the phone.

"Will you please stay with my daughter?" her mom asked the man. "How is she? How is her boyfriend Paul?"

"I don't think he's in good shape, but I will stay with your daughter and let you know as soon as we find out which hospital she is going to."

Jacqui allowed herself to feel a small sliver of relief. At least someone knew where she was. It's going to be OK. Again she surveyed the area trying to locate her friends and see where they were going. It's second nature for all of them to look out for each other. She just wished she could do more than just watch from the sidelines.

She saw Paul being hoisted into an ambulance. He still looked like he wasn't so badly hurt for some reason. Maybe his injuries were not even as extensive as hers, she thought. That would be a miracle since she had seen that JP was in bad shape. With Paul's anxiety, she hoped she was right. He didn't need to deal with the stress of something like this. She couldn't wait for all of this to be over.

She heard someone talk about the possibility that there may be more bombs in the city, but before she could even think about that, a different police officer came up and said, "I can take her in my cruiser. Can we carry her?"

"No, I can walk if you help me," Jacqui said. They got on each side of her and guided her as she hobbled toward the awaiting cruiser parked on Ring Road. As they helped Jacqui to the car, they looked at her bare back peeking through the blanket and then at each other.

There was the image of distinct handprints outlined in the soot and charred skin.

***

After the police redirected the runners away from the finish line, Mike Jefferson just stood still for a few minutes watching as smoke curled up into the blue sky over Boston. He had heard the second explosion clearly even with his headphones on and knew something was wrong. With nowhere else to go, Mike headed away from the chaos up ahead. He decided to backtrack and see if he could locate his father somewhere along the course.

He passed a state police station that his father had worked at years ago when Mike was just a little kid. He hoped that was a sign that he would find his family soon and figure out what was happening. About a half hour later, he saw a familiar car pass by. Out hopped his mother and his aunt. They had just come from the finish line and were covered in blood. Mike wasn't sure what they had been through, but if they were all right, at least that means his friends are OK too.

"You need to find Paul," his mother said to him. Then Mike spotted his father driving up in the police cruiser. His head started spinning. What was going on? Where was Paul, JP, and the rest of the gang? Before he could think too much about it, he jumped into the car with his father and both cars made their way home. After hearing what had happened, Mike was on edge. Fortunately, his family was unharmed for the most part, but where was everyone else? No one seemed to know exactly what had happened to the group after the explosion. The next logical place to look was one of the numerous hospitals in Boston.

Mike's dad didn't want to leave his wife in such a fragile state, but she insisted that he go ahead and take Mike back to the city and to the hospital. He needed to check on his friends. They are like family and they're going to need him. Grateful, but unsure of what he would find, Mike rode in silence as the police cruiser sliced through traffic in search of the Nordens.

CHAPTER 3 – RESCUE

Across town, EMTs Matt O'Connor and Sean Gelinas were sitting in their ambulance stationed at Boston College, expecting to handle minor issues like dizziness, intoxication, or other residual effects of Patriot's Day celebrations at the colleges in the area. Then dispatch radioed that they were to head over to Boston University, about three miles away. Matt was driving and Sean rode shotgun as they made their way along the crowded streets. They ended up on Boylston and found themselves stuck in traffic. Just then a man in a car beside them rolled down his window.

"Have you guys heard anything about a bomb?" he yelled.

"No, not a thing," Sean responded. Curious, they decided they'd better investigate. Matt called a friend of his who lives farther up on Boylston to see if she knew anything. She didn't, but she had just seen at least 15 police cruisers zoom by, all lit up. It seemed unusual to have that many at once.

Meanwhile, Sean checked with dispatch to see if they had any updates but, again, they came up empty. No sooner had Sean replaced the radio on its hook when they got a call to respond to an explosion on Boylston. Once they heard the location, Matt

42

instantly realized they were only about one minute away. As they fired up the siren and made their way through the traffic, Matt noticed the bright blue sky ahead. It looked so peaceful and serene that he thought the call must be about an insignificant explosion.

As they got to the scene, the air had suddenly and without warning turned dark gray. The smoke was thick and omnipresent, the coppery smell of blood and flesh invading their sense of smell. It was as if they had entered an alternate world, one that had seemed to change in an instant to darkness and mayhem. They saw groups of people huddled around bodies sprawled along the road and sidewalks.

Just as Matt was trying to decide where to park, he saw a firefighter flagging him down. As they came to a stop, Sean jumped out and a man pleaded with him, "Tourniquets, do you guys have tourniquets?" He'd never heard such a sense of urgency; he knew it was serious. As he gathered the supplies, the man grabbed them and ran. Then others started reaching for bandages directly out of the ambulance. Sean and Matt looked ahead of them and they both saw Paul already situated on a backboard and restlessly awaiting transport. The guys quickly went into rescue mode and took note of the victim. His leg had been severed above the knee and someone had attached a crude but effective belt-tourniquet to the upper thigh. They left him on the backboard and placed it on the stretcher, easing their patient into the back of the ambulance.

Matt hopped back into the driver's seat and they were directed to go to Boston Medical Center, but Beth Israel Deaconess Medical Center was the closest, and probably the easiest to reach. Before he took off, Matt briefly considered trying to take another patient or two, but it was obvious their current charge was in serious need of attention and would likely die if they waited much longer. He decided to transport this victim as quickly as possible and then return to the scene.

As he carefully created a path through the crowd, Sean rode in the back and assessed Paul's wounds.

"Here," Paul said shoving his cell phone to Sean, "Talk to my mom."

"Hello," Sean said hesitantly.

"What's going on?" Liz Brown-Norden asked excitedly. "What's happening?"

"Well, he's right, ma'am. I heard him tell you he's hurt bad, but we're taking him to the hospital now." He informed her that they had been able to stop the bleeding with a tourniquet and suddenly there was silence.

With that he passed the phone back to Paul. There was no time to waste; he needed to ensure that his patient would survive the ride to the hospital. He looked at Paul's right leg and saw that while the stump was still bleeding, the belt seemed to be holding a majority of the blood back. He knew not to disturb that situation. There were too many unknowns, too much risk.

He saw that the detached limb had been placed on the board and flipped round, pointing at an awkward, unnatural angle. His first thought was to address the foot that was partially severed from the detached part of the leg, but realized that was not necessary. It was just instinctive to dress the wounds. As he cut off Paul's shirt to examine his chest for injury, he consoled the surprisingly calm young man.

"How am I?" he asked. "Am I going to die? Did I lose my leg?"

Sean didn't want to upset him. "It's going to be alright. We're on the way to the hospital. You're not going to die." Despite his reassurances, Sean really wasn't certain. This was the most extreme trauma he had seen thus far in his career. All he could do was focus on the patient and do his best.

After a bit of silence, Paul asked again, "Did I lose my leg?"

"Yes," Sean finally told him. "You did, but you're not going to die. Just hang on."

And he did. Sean watched as his patient became surprisingly calm, only asking a few more questions. "Where's my brother? He was with me. Did you see him?"

"There are lots of people on the scene. Your brother is in good hands." Sean hoped he was right. He worked busily to dress the burns and search for any visible signs of shrapnel or other foreign objects. He couldn't see any head trauma, which was a good thing, but he couldn't ignore the second-degree burns that disfigured his skin. He checked the left leg and saw that it had been mangled as well, but at least it was not severed.

Ensuring that his patient didn't die en route to the hospital was his sole focus. *I don't want to be the last person this guy ever talks to,* Sean thought. Surprisingly, Paul wasn't complaining of pain or discomfort. Sean couldn't believe that he wasn't in severe shock or crying out in agony. After Sean had reassured him that things would be OK, he seemed to be deep in thought, possibly processing the events that had just occurred.

Matt continued driving, using the speakers on the ambulance to address the crowd and get them to clear the way. As they eased the ambulance into the emergency entrance of Beth Israel, Matt saw tents going up along the grounds to manage the casualties they were anticipating. Matt and Sean quickly wheeled Paul to the OR and watched as the medical team took over—cutting off the remaining partially burned clothes and quickly assessing the medical condition of their trauma patient.

Outside of the hospital, the duo attempted to clean out the back of the ambulance before heading back to the scene. Blood coated the sides and floor. They tried to decontaminate the area, but there was too much blood and tissue. Every time they put down a sheet, it quickly turned to crimson red, soaking up the blood that seemed never-ending. With time ticking away, they decided it would have to do. They needed to get back to the scene to help the others.

On the ride back to Boylston, Sean tried to process what had just happened. His training had certainly prepared him well. He had never expected to come across such extreme trauma today, but he had gotten through it. He had only expected to see maybe a case of dehydration, foot injuries, possibly even a heart attack, but not this. It all seemed like some intense dream with no end.

**

After growing up on the South Shore, James "Jimma" Allen lived in Boston for over ten years working as a paramedic before moving to the small community of Medford, a town adjacent to Stoneham. His current unit is located in a police station, unlike other communities that typically house paramedics and EMTs at firehouses.

His current shift was 4:00 p.m. to midnight, which was a lot better than his previous 4:00 p.m. to 2:00 a.m. slot. Jimma and his partner were working a double shift on April 15 to help with the Boston Marathon and all of the craziness that often occurs on Patriot's Day. They had been assigned as a field transport unit at Boylston and Hereford Streets where they were parked with doors open, facing down Boylston alongside a small tent where people could receive basic medical treatment. They were there to transport from tent to the hospital on the rare occasions that it became necessary.

At around 2:00 that day, his partner was scanning the menu of The Capital Grille, thinking about what they would treat themselves to for lunch. It was a special day and they wanted some good food. Jimma was easing into the long shift and listening to Pearl Jam on his headphones as he thought about what he would order. Just ahead, Jimma saw the smoke from the first blast. He jabbed his partner with his elbow. "You see that?"

"Yeah, what do you think it is?"

"I don't know, but—" Jimma was stopped mid-sentence as the second explosion ripped through the air, this time only about 1½ blocks away. He instinctively snapped a picture with his phone and they both scrambled out of the truck and onto the street. Over 30 firefighters and other emergency personnel were gathered outside of the nearly fire station and Jimma watched as they all leapt into action, heading into the ominous fog of soot and blood, unconcerned with their own safety.

The paramedic duo hopped back in their truck and fortuitously saw a cruiser making its way to the scene. They quickly got behind and followed the car around the block, up Exeter Street and back on to Boylston, now right on the scene. The cruiser pulled off to the side of the road and the ambulance pressed forward until they met with hoards of people clogging the street. The pedestrians yelled at them for help and began banging on the hood. They knew this was a serious situation. Just then a police officer approached them carrying an injured 3-year-old with head trauma.

"Guys, you've got to take this one in your truck. I'm going back to the scene."

With trained expedience, they eased the child into the back of the idling ambulance. Seconds later an older couple approached them.

"My wife needs help," the man said.

"OK, we can take her. Your injuries aren't as extensive. You can get treatment at the finish line. Let's go!"

As Jimma got the woman situated, he felt the truck moving. They were going closer to the scene of the blast to try and see if anyone else needed to be transported quickly. With the child secured, Jimma and the dazed woman held on as the doors flapped back and forth. Soon they were parked directly in front of The Forum Restaurant as the second unit to arrive on site. The responders that had leapt into action at the fire station were already expertly managing the scene.

In the back of the ambulance, Jimma continued to get his patients assessed and situated for the ride to the hospital. The woman was in intense pain with obvious burns all over her body. The child was lying toward the back. There had been crying for a few minutes, but now there was only silence. Shock had likely taken hold. As Jimma continued to dress the woman's wounds and reassure the child, the doors burst open as his partner grabbed supplies to handle the trauma on the ground.

Once his charges were sufficiently managed, Jimma jumped out of the truck to see if he could help on the scene. What he saw was sheer pandemonium as the rescuers scrambled to stabilize victims while pedestrians ran by, obviously unsure where to go. He watched as first responders and helpful bystanders worked furiously to stabilize the tragically wounded. The ground in front of him was littered with fingers, toes, tissue, and blood—in fact the street was covered in the sticky red substance. It was almost too much to take in. He realized he needed to stay with the truck.

He knew that they were assigning colors to the victims as part of the mass casualty triage procedure. Green, priority 3, is for the ones not seriously injured, sometimes called the "walking wounded." Yellow is a priority 2 for moderate to serious injuries. Red is priority 1, serious and life-threatening injuries. Reds are of course first priority for treatment and transportation. Consequently, black is assigned to those who are found at the scene with no vital signs.

Back in the truck, Jimma waited until another driver got assigned to take the truck to the hospital since his partner was involved at the scene. He returned to his patients and set up IV bags for the child. The back doors snapped open and his partner was standing there covered in soot and the strong, unmistakable odor of burning flesh.

"This kid's cutting the line. He's gotta get in there."

"Where do you want me to put him?" Jimma asked. He was reluctant to take on more passengers and compromise the ones he already had. "Never mind," Jimma decided after seen the victim. "We'll find room!"

Because the young man was in a scoop basket set on a longboard, it wouldn't quite fit. That was made for transition to a gurney, not for transport, but there was no time to waste. The paramedics helped the woman move to the side and they jammed it into a space that was a bit too small. They knew time was crucial for this guy's survival. With the back doors closed once again, Jimma was alone with the three victims and he immediately began to assess his newest.

"What's your name?" he asked the guy.

"Joseph Paul. JP Norden," he gasped.

"How old are you?" Jimma asked. He knew he had a priority 1 on his hands and he wanted to keep him talking.

"33."

"Listen. You're fucked up," Jimma leveled with him. "You're gonna live, but you're fucked up. We're going to get you squared away. We're going to get you to the hospital, but I want you to know you have a lot of trauma. You're missing a leg. I just want you to know what you're dealing with."

JP went silent as he processed this information. As he watched Jimma moving around, he looked over and saw the woman on the other side and she was in obvious pain. Then he heard the child screaming, and then silence.

As Jimma continued talking to him and reassuring him, a comforting sense of calm snaked through JP's body like ether. He could feel himself relax now that he was away from the chaos on the sidewalk and this paramedic was cleaning him up and dressing his wounds. But he could tell that the ambulance hadn't moved.

"When are we leaving?" he asked.

"We are waiting for a driver," Jimma said.

"What the hell do you mean we don't have a driver? I don't understand why we aren't leaving."

"It's all right. Stop worrying. Someone is coming. You just need to take it easy. As soon as we get one, we're out of here. I promise."

JP sighed and tried to relax.

"Typically I would put an IV in you, but I don't think I can."

"Why not?" JP asked.

Jimma didn't respond. He didn't want to tell him that he couldn't find a vein. The skin was too burned and coated with soot to safely insert a needle. As he continued administering care, he realized JP had gone quiet on him.

"You alright down there," Jimma said as he tried to manage the woman's bleeding.

"Yeah, I'm OK," JP said softly. "I'm really dizzy though."

"It's all right, man. You've lost a lot of blood, but we going to take care of you. Just hang in there."

Jimma saw him relax a bit and he realized JP seemed to be in much worse shape than the other two. He must have been very close to that explosion. His hair was singed and gray ash and pungent soot caked his body. His clothes were burned beyond belief. The makeshift tourniquet on his right leg went all the way from his upper thigh to the missing part of his lower leg. There was no blood coming from the stump, just charred, protruding bone. Then he looked at the left leg. The pants were mostly singed off and the thigh was filleted wide open from hip to knee.

Then Jimma noticed an oval key ring resting on JP's upper thigh. He gave it a tug to remove it and then he realized the other keys attached to it were buried in his flesh. JP let out a scream of pain. Jimma quickly let go and apologized. He made an attempt to get a blood pressure reading, but it was impossible due to the extent of the injuries and the other noise in the back of the ambulance. He put an oxygen mask on JP's face to help him relax, clear his lungs, and manage his breathing. Then he set out to repair the temporary tourniquet and apply dressing to the trauma area, anything he could do to prepare his patient for the awaiting medical staff.

When they arrived at the hospital, Jimma stayed with JP while the others were offloaded. Then he wheeled JP to room 54 at Brigham and Women's Hospital, gave the staff a quick download of what he had observed and in seconds they were heading back to the site.

The nurse on duty asked JP who they could contact. He thought for a minute, but all of the numbers are programmed in his phone—wherever that is now. He couldn't remember. Then one of them came to him. He told them to call his girlfriend, Kelly.

As he headed back to the marathon, Jimma thought about how JP's eyes had followed him during the entire ride. It was like he was determined not to blackout, not to give in. He displayed a strong will that is rare with that kind of blast trauma. Surprisingly his hearing seemed functional because he responded to questions. How a kid like that held on with so much blood loss was an amazing testament to the human spirit. It was the part of the job that always surprised Jimma—how strong people can be when their life depends on it.

***

While JP and Paul were being loaded into separate ambulances, Jacqui was walking cautiously to the awaiting police cruiser and watching the interaction between the man helping her and the police officer.

"What hospital are you taking her to?" the man asked. "I promised I'd call her mother and let her know."

"Boston Medical Center."

The man turned to Jacqui. "I'm calling your mom now."

As the police car reached Huntington Avenue, Jacqui saw an ambulance ahead. The policeman flagged them down and hopped out of his car, leaving Jacqui in the backseat. "Can you take her to the hospital?" he asked, pointing to his car.

Soon she found herself in the back of the ambulance barreling down the street, ending up at Tufts Medical Center. Even though it had only been a few blocks away, it took a long time to make their way because all of the streets were closed due to the lockdown and threats of more possible explosions. Pain started to take over her body.

"Can you give me any medicine?" she pleaded with the attendant. "It really hurts."

"Sorry," he responded. "They have to ask you some questions first at the hospital—allergies and that kind of thing. Hang on. We'll be there soon."

As they rode along in silence, Jacqui was worried that she couldn't feel her fingers, so she kept making a fist over and over to try and convince herself that her hands were normal. The pain was excruciating, but she couldn't stop squeezing.

CHAPTER 4 - PAUL

At around 3:05 on April 15, Liz received the call she had dreaded since she first gave birth in 1979. "Ma, I'm hurt real bad," she heard her son, Paul, say. His voice had such a strange, plaintive tone, unlike anything she had heard from him before. It sent chills down her spine. Her head began spinning.

"Where's JP?" she managed to ask.

"I don't know where JP and Jacqui are! I can't find them!"

Sean Gelinas took the phone from Paul. "Hello, he's going to be all right. We were able to stop the bleeding with a tourniquet—"

Liz had taken the phone outside to get a better signal. As she heard that word the phone slid out of her hand and bounced on the ground like a coin.

Earlier that morning, she and Paul had been hanging out leisurely in the living room of her second-story walkup talking about the upcoming college football season. It was such a nice Boston spring day that everyone was making plans. Paul hadn't been totally sure if he and Jacqui were going to watch Mike run the marathon. He wasn't excited about the crowd, but Mike was a long-time friend of the whole family, so they wanted to show their

54

support. JP had planned to go and Jonathan might go with Paul; it just depended on how everyone felt that day. Little sister, Caitlin, was working downtown at her boyfriend's restaurant in anticipation of the flood of customers from Fenway Park located nearby.

Liz had plans of her own. She and her oldest daughter, Colleen, and her granddaughter, Gabbie, were going off to pay some bills and do some grocery shopping. It was a nice day to take care of some errands and spend time with family. First, she stopped by to visit her brother Peter—or Uncle Pete as most everyone calls him. "The boys are at the marathon," she told him. Peter told her that his daughter went too, with some friends. Pete's wife was going to the mall. Everyone was taking advantage of the accommodating weather.

After leaving her brother's house, Liz, Colleen, and little Gabbie were off to the store. Liz decided to get the kind of chicken that JP likes. That would entice him to come over for dinner after he and his friends finish up at the marathon. Since he was living away from home, she took every opportunity to bring everyone together.

She also wanted to make sure she got something Paul likes to avoid the good-natured teasing she would get about treating JP as the favorite. Paul loves Nutty Buddy ice cream so she picked some up for him. They share the running joke that JP is the special one, probably because he's the first born (and probably because it drives Liz crazy), but like most mothers she has the natural ability to make each of her kids feel special and unique. Raising them outside of the big city was probably one of the best decisions she's ever made.

***

Once known as "The Friendly Town," Stoneham is one of the many bedroom communities just outside of Boston. Medford, Woburn, Wakefield, and many other areas about ten miles away from Beantown provide a suburban lifestyle for families looking for a slower life just outside of the bustling downtown.

Today, the population of Stoneham is around 21,000 and there is still only one middle school and one high school. The local newspaper proudly features columns that highlight local potluck suppers and pothole repairs along Main Street. Having Interstates 93 and 95 in close proximity means residents can commute to Boston and surrounding cities with relative ease. With one theater and mostly locally owned restaurants, the atmosphere is familial and New England-y.

The Brown family settled in Stoneham during the '60s and '70s and loved the small town feel that was evident as folks headed to the local stores that dotted Main Street every weekend for shopping and socializing. Good schools, a relatively low crime rate, and close proximity to highways gave the Brown parents confidence that their children would learn the importance of family and community, just as they had while surviving The Great Depression, when family was all most people had.

Liz grew up with a sister and three brothers, and she was especially close with her parents. They enjoyed a stable, modest life that may have lacked in luxuries, but made up for it in family unity. With a father who worked in middle management, and a stay-at-home mother, money was usually tight for the seven of them. Holidays and celebrations were meager, with the exception of Christmas. Somehow, and to the amazement of the kids, the

Browns managed to make that one day of the year an extravagant one—at least as far as they were concerned.

Naturally, being a small town, the children grew up knowing most everyone in the community since they all attended middle and high school together. Liz especially liked the quaint charm of the area and the familiarity of the place where she grew up. It was a place where the kids played outside until the streetlights came on—the universal sign that it was time for dinner. Then they had a couple more hours of street ball or flashlight tag before heading inside for the night.

Liz was especially close to her brother Peter and sister, Cheryl, growing up. While Liz was more on the reserved side, Peter was an outgoing and popular football player, and Cheryl was a no-nonsense, well-liked girl. Brand names were a luxury for the Browns, so when Peter got a couple pair of corduroy Levi's, Liz could often be seen wearing them around the halls of Stoneham High. Eager for a grown-up life, Liz visited her brother often when he went off to college on a football scholarship—the cost of a post-secondary education being prohibitive for many Stoneham families.

In the late 1970s, at the age of 17, Liz was a senior in high school when she found herself faced with a grown-up issue. She was pregnant. While eventual motherhood had never been a question for her, she certainly hadn't planned on it happening before graduation. However, she knew that while it may not have been the perfect scenario, her family would support her decision and help out. It's what they were all about.

Her first son, Joseph Paul Norden, was born on October 12, 1979 and affectionately dubbed JP to avoid confusion with his father. During the 1980's, Liz had four more children. Paul was born in Stoneham in June of '81 and Jonathan came along in '85. In '87, her first daughter, Colleen, was born and finally Caitlin, the baby, made her debut in '88. Throughout the "me" decade, Liz and her boyfriend were on and off as they moved around in a five-mile radius of their hometown to various apartments, duplexes, and single-family homes. They eventually married in 1984, but the union was never the traditional married life Liz had envisioned.

Early on, Liz realized that she would need to be the stabilizing force for her children, and with the help of her supportive parents and siblings, she did just that. For Liz, her dreams were never limited by the size of her bank account. Despite having to live in government-subsidizing house for a while and sometimes applying for assistance to make ends meet, she knew as long as her kids witnessed her work ethic and realized the value of a strong, supportive family, they would have the foundation necessary to create fulfilling lives of their own someday.

Fast-forward to 2013. It seems like Liz's parenting has paid off. The passing of her parents a decade ago was difficult for everyone and the children never stop missing their doting grandparents. Paul had developed an especially close relationship with his grandmother, a bond that Liz encouraged as it seemed to help him with his natural shyness. However, by sticking together and depending on each other, they had all safely, for the most part, eased into adulthood unscathed.

The Norden house (wherever it happened to be) always became the social hub of the neighborhood, sort of the sun around which friends orbit like happy planets. Local kids know it is a safe, loving environment where they can hang out with the Norden brood and be themselves. Liz Brown-Norden has always been happy with the situation because that means she always knows where her children are at all times. Being referred to as the resident "cool mom" doesn't hurt either.

Her natural ability to make anyone feel comfortable and welcome is common knowledge in Stoneham. When you are at the Nordens', you are just like family. Holidays and family occasions are never restricted—friends are always welcome to drop by, and they do. Everyone knows how Liz loves holidays, especially Christmas, and never fails to indulge her kids as much as she can.

Within her family, she has always been careful to make her each of them feel special, no matter what. Even though they joke that JP is the favorite, it's easy to see that her devotion is not divided unevenly. When her kids fight with each other, they quickly make up, and if someone outside of the family feels like adding their two cents, they are quickly shut down. There's a clear mandate that family comes first. Friends are very important, but family is the core.

It was important to create an atmosphere of camaraderie because Mom was often working various jobs to make ends meet— office assistant, grocery clerk, anything to keep the bills paid. As a protective parent, Liz has always been a worrier. It is just in her nature to be concerned with any of her kids being out too late or not being where they said they were going. No matter where she was working, she was still calling them, even as adults, to see if they arrived safely and when they would be home.

As the oldest, JP and Paul often found themselves watching after their siblings and providing a male influence as they grew up. Being protective of their younger brother and two sisters, JP became especially adept at dispensing advice with Paul acting as more of a sounding board for the others. They were quick to defend each other if necessary as they became a tight, insular group while their mother was often away trying to generate income for the family as best she could.

During the spring of 2013, JP had been living in his own apartment for a few years while the others shared space in a small 2nd floor apartment in nearby Wakefield. The Nordens continued to eke out a modest, small-town existence despite the crippling effects of the recession and the always challenging job market.

They found themselves following the familiar blue-collar pattern of most of their friends as they secured entry-level labor or service industry jobs. Over the years, they would find themselves in the familiar routine of working long hours for meager pay each week, until Friday night when they had a reprieve until the next Monday. Weekends were theirs to head to the bars and hang with friends as they created lasting memories, and the occasional hangover.

Now young adults, the Nordens had begun forging their own way and receiving small paychecks of their own that would help with household expenses. They may not be rich in a financial sense, but they can afford to pay their bills (mostly on time), and have a little left over for some fun. For this tight-knit Stoneham group, that's enough.

***

During her shopping trip on marathon day, Liz decided that she'd better text the boys before they made plans. With that group of friends hanging around in Boston, they might all gather for dinner there instead of coming back to Wakefield. She sent a group text to Paul and JP telling them to come to dinner for some chicken and Nutty Buddy ice cream. Then her phone died. The text wouldn't go through. She decided she would re-charge at home and then send it.

While Liz was shopping, Colleen had gotten dozens of calls from Caitlin. With her battery on low, she decided she would talk to her later. Finally after continuous calls, she decided to answer. Sisters can be so annoying.

Caitlin said, "There was a bomb at the marathon!"

"Ok," said Colleen. "And..?" It was certainly unfortunate, but she knows her sister can be dramatic at times; she has hopes of a career in entertainment after all.

"Do you know if Paul and the others are there?" Caitlin asked.

"Caitlin," Colleen said, "There are a million people there. Nothing's going to happen to them."

Already in downtown Boston, Caitlin was in a panic. Since the restaurant was slammed because of the game that day, she had offered to make a few deliveries. While she was driving, the restaurant called her to tell her to make sure she didn't go near Newbury Street. Then her boyfriend called and said there are bombs in the area.

Caitlin was totally confused. Bombs? In Boston? Her brothers and their friends were at the marathon right now! She quickly tried to reach her mom but as usual, Liz's phone was dead. Frustrated she tried both of her brothers. No answer. She kept calling her sister Colleen over and over. *Where the hell is everyone*, she thought, dialing Colleen's number again.

Once done with grocery shopping, Liz and Colleen made their way home. Liz went upstairs to see who was still there and saw her husband watching TV. He comes by frequently to see his kids and spend time with Gabbie. Today, he had planned to take his granddaughter to the playground while Colleen went to work out at the gym.

"Hey, Liz," he yelled, "a bomb went off at the Boston Marathon."

"What? You're kidding me. I think all of the boys are there."

Liz went back downstairs. Paul was nowhere to be found. He had told her that if he was gone, he and Jacqui had probably gone to the marathon. "Paul left his car here, but not his keys," Liz said. "It's weird. He never goes to the marathon."

Colleen's phone rang and she handed it to Liz. "Ma, it's Caitlin. She needs to talk to you." Liz took the phone hesitantly. She didn't have a good feeling about this. Everything seemed to be off for some reason—Paul's car still here, an explosion at the marathon, it didn't feel right.

"Ma," Caitlin said, "a bomb went off!"

"I know," Liz said as calmly as she knew how. "I'm going to try and call the boys now." Liz gave Colleen the phone and headed to the kitchen to charge hers, put away the groceries, and call the boys. She heard the door slam and realized both her husband and Colleen had headed out of the house.

She thought she was alone and began searching for her charger when her youngest son, Jonathan, came running into the room. "Ma, Paul's on the phone!" Startled, she took the phone outside to get a better signal. After Liz heard the word *tourniquet*, she quickly felt light-headed. As the phone dropped to the ground, her head began spinning. What was going on? Where was everyone? She was in the exact predicament she had hoped would never take place. She always feared *the* phone call and now here it was. She heard Jonathan talking on the phone, telling someone that they were on the way.

Colleen was driving to the gym when she got a panicked call from Jonathan telling her she needed to get back home fast. She could tell from his voice something was wrong, so she turned around. As she pulled up to the house she saw her mother leaning over, getting sick in the yard, Jonathan standing nearby. She jumped out of the car and Liz ran back inside to change clothes, hers now a splattered mess, not to mention the Pollack-like image she had left in the driveway.

As they quickly headed into town, Jonathan drove as Liz and Colleen frantically tried to call and text anyone they could think of. This day had suddenly come off its hinges, gone sideways. It was such an unsettling feeling. As they were driving they realized they hadn't found out which hospital to go to, and Boston has lots of them. They tried calling every hospital they could think of, but because of all of the commotion, no one actually had a list of patient names yet. And if they did, they were not able to release that information. Liz was in a panic when she talked to a woman at Mass General who was so nice it helped her calm down for a second. "There is no Norden at our hospital at this time."

Uncle Pete had turned on the TV to check out who won the Red Sox game and to get an update on the marathon. Just then the first explosion happened. Then another quickly followed. He immediately started calling his family. He contacted his wife and told her to get home, but she didn't have a ride, so he immediately went to the mall to get her. He tracked down his daughter and to his relief she hadn't gone to the marathon after all, so he insisted she come home quickly. He let out a sigh of relief, but hadn't Liz said something about the boys being there?

Meanwhile, Caitlin was at the restaurant working her phone. She was determined to find out what was going on. She called Paul's number over and over and finally a strange voice answered.

"Hello," Caitlin said hesitantly. This wasn't Jacqui so who was on Paul's phone? "I'm trying to find my brother Paul."

"He's here," the woman said. "He's in very serious condition." "What?" Caitlin said. "Where's 'here?'"

"Beth Israel Hospital."

Caitlin did not have a good feeling about this. "Is JP there too?"

"I'm sorry, I'm not sure. It's very busy here right now."

Caitlin ran to the men's room to get her boyfriend. There was no time to waste. "Come out here!" she yelled.

"What's up?"

"I just found out Paul is at the hospital!"

"Ok, just relax."

"No, this is bad."

With the minutes ticking by, Caitlin hurried to the car as her boyfriend slid into the driver's seat. Beth Israel was only about five minutes away in normal traffic, but she felt a sense of pride as she watched him blow through every red light, determined to get her to the hospital as fast as possible. After going to the wrong entrance, they quickly found the emergency room. As one of the first relatives to arrive, social workers and other hospital personnel surrounded her, eager to get information on one of their patients who was too disfigured for them to identify.

"Can I see Paul?" she asked to no one in particular.

"No, he's in surgery. You'll have to wait in here," came the answer.

At least she knew one of her brothers had been located, but she realized it was just her and her boyfriend there. Where was everyone else? She quickly called her mom to tell her they needed to come to Beth Israel.

Liz was grateful when she got the call. They had parked the car and were at Boston Medical trying to determine if either of the Norden brothers were there. She had spoken to one of her sons and he had told her he was hurt real bad. It was tearing her up inside. She felt the pain and uncertainly of not knowing where her children were, what had happened to them. She couldn't get the word *bomb* out of her head. "That was Caitlin," she told the others. "Paul is at Beth Israel!"

They headed out into the street to locate the car they had hastily parked in the only space they had found. As the three of them walked along the road, they began to pick up their pace until they were literally running, desperately searching for the car. Liz was crying so hard she could barely see in front of her. The roads were blocked off, they couldn't get their bearings. They weren't sure how they were going to get to Beth Israel. There were no cabs around and it was much too far to walk. If they got in the car, they weren't sure they'd be able to get through.

"Get off the street! Get inside of a building!" a cop yelled. People were encouraged to go into any store or shop and clear the streets because bomb scares were rampant across the city. Liz looked up and saw they were in front of a random bakery on Commonwealth Avenue.

She turned to her kids. "I'm getting to the hospital. I'm not just going to wait around in one of these buildings." Liz ran over to the cop that had yelled at them.

"Ma'am, you have to get off the street!"

"My son is at Beth Israel Hospital, and I've got to get there!" Her determination was unmistakable.

"Get in your car. We'll escort you to the hospital, otherwise you'll never make it."

As they piled in, Liz thought more about the bomb. What did that mean? Like a little pipe bomb? Fireworks? She just couldn't imagine what that had to do with Paul being at the hospital. It didn't make sense, but then again nothing seemed to make sense that day. As they traveled along in the car, she saw the unmistakably dazed look of tourists and visitors as they tried to figure out where to go in their unfamiliar surroundings. Even with the police escort, it felt like an eternity until they finally arrived at the hospital. Liz was determined to see her son and still worried about where JP was. Not hearing anything yet, she feared the worst, but she wouldn't dare say it. Not yet.

As they approached Beth Israel, there were more people crowded along the roads and traffic was thicker. Obviously they were closer to whatever had happened. It was slow going, but the National Guard was moving barricades to allow the small convoy to pass through. The cop had told them to stay close, and Liz looked over at her son and saw him focused on the road ahead, not letting that cruiser get more than a few feet away from them. She was glad he was doing the driving. She looked back and saw that another vehicle had jumped in behind them, making use of the pathway they were creating. It was practically the only way to traverse the congested roads.

It was around 4:30 when they pulled up in front of the hospital. A valet opened the door for them and they hurried to the emergency room. The place was in lockdown mode with security swarming the halls and everyone crowded in the lobby along with chaplains, social workers, and other medical personnel. They were gathering information and trying to identify the patients that had already arrived, naturally without any clue about their identities.

Caitlin was so glad to finally see some familiar faces as she had been patiently waiting for more word on Paul's condition. They were all told they would just need to get comfortable. Liz was still frantic trying to locate her other son. While finding Paul had certainly eased her anxiety level, she had such an ominous feeling about JP. If she knew her boys, they were hanging out together. So if this happened to Paul, where could JP be? She hated to even let the thought cloud her brain, but she couldn't stop it.

As she watched the others continue calling their network of friends to try and find out more information, she sat down for a rest. While she caught her breath she looked down and saw she had on one pink sock, one gray sock, black stretch pants, and a gray-purple-black sweater. What the hell? She looked like she'd dressed herself in the dark. Luckily she had remembered her purse, because security was tight and they were checking IDs of everyone who came into the hospital. She could tell there was a lot more to this than she had even imagined. It made sense that the police would be involved, but she also saw intense-looking people with FBI emblems on their jackets.

The family knew Paul was there, but since he hadn't been officially identified, they still couldn't get any medical information. Very few of the patients had been entered into the system because the staff had gone quickly into life-saving mode. They would put names with faces later, but it was difficult for those waiting in the hallways for any tidbit of news about their loved one's condition.

During this time, Mike Jefferson had been furiously calling anyone and everyone he knew trying to locate his friends. He knew from what his mother had told him that Paul and JP had taken the brunt of the blast. It wouldn't be good news. However, he finally got in contact with his cousin, a nurse at Beth Israel. She knows Paul and recognized him right away. She told Mike that he was there. It was around 6:00 when Mike called Jonathan's phone. He didn't realize Liz had answered. He wasn't paying that much attention. He had news to deliver.

"Jonathan, I don't know how you're going to tell your mom this, but I just found out Paul's going to have his leg amputated right now."

Liz had been pacing back and forth, holding her son's phone and hoping for news. All of a sudden, she was in a crumpled pile on the hard floor of the waiting room. A chaplain and several others rushed over to help.

At around 7:00, another call came in. Someone had located Kelly, JP's girlfriend, at Brigham and Women's Hospital just three blocks away.

JP was in surgery.

CHAPTER 5 – JP

With a little over 700 students in grades 9-12, everyone who attends Stoneham High School knows each other. So when Kelly Castine transferred there after her father was stationed in Iraq, she made friends quickly. She had been living in Woburn, not too far away, so she knew some of the kids already.

Pretty, popular, and outgoing, she had little trouble acclimating to her new environment. She and Jonathan Norden became fast friends and as it usually happens, when you know one Norden, you eventually know all of them. So of course Kelly met the other siblings, and a natural connection sparked with one of them. After high school graduation, she moved into a small apartment in Stoneham and in December of 2010 she and JP began dating.

They are a striking couple, JP with his approachable good looks and Kelly with her small, toned frame and long, dark hair. It was an instant and natural attraction since their personalities mesh nicely. Both are very gregarious and outgoing, spending weekends with large groups of friends either together or going off with their own crew and then meeting up later. Comedy shows, dinner, dancing, hanging out at the bar—they are rarely just sitting around at home. But when they do, it is usually at Kelly's place. They both feel comfortable there and it is more well-appointed than JP's bachelor pad where the refrigerator often contains little more than Bud Light and a mangled bottle of mustard.

Sunday, April 14, 2013 was a typical Sunday for the young couple. They had gone to a restaurant called Artichokes in Wakefield. It's a little fancier than the places they usually go, but it was the day before Patriot's Day and since Kelly would likely have to work, they couldn't go to the marathon together. Plus, JP wanted to get his favorite meal—the steak and pepper plate.

He liked it so much that one time Kelly had tried to recreate it in her kitchen at home. The results were lackluster and barely resembled the restaurant dish, but like a good boyfriend JP had eaten it and assured her that it was tasty. She knew better, but appreciated the gesture. "You'll eat anything," she told him with a smile.

The next morning JP was still shaking off the cloudiness of sleep, as Kelly got dressed for work. She leaned over to kiss him goodbye before leaving her apartment.

"Bye. Have fun at the marathon," she told him, not even trying to hide her jealousy. "I might try to bring the kids there. So maybe I will get to go after all. I just have to check with their mom." Then she reached over and rubbed his legs, a habit she had developed because she hated having to leave when he was able to stay in bed. She would rather hang out with him, but she has to pay the rent.

Her job as a nanny is flexible and is helping her to earn money while she takes classes to be a medical assistant. She knows it will take a little time, but she's always had a knack for taking care of people and a steady, dependable career would be better than scrambling for babysitting work for the rest of her life.

Currently, she was taking care of two children, a 6-year-old girl and 2-year-old boy. They're good kids and she genuinely likes childcare because they like to play and be active, which is perfect for her. Of course the little girl was out of school because of Patriot's Day so Kelly had told her boss that if things went well maybe she could take them to watch the marathon. Plenty of her friends would be there so there would be lots of help if she needed it. And the kids would probably get a kick out of all the excitement.

The week before, that had been fine, but on Monday the little girl wasn't feeling well. Her mom asked Kelly to keep her at home, something Kelly certainly agreed with even though it meant she would be cooped up inside. She was a little bummed to be missing out on the beautiful day and all of her friends hanging out on Boylston, but she switched gears and settled in with the little ones. JP had gone back to sleep, but he called her later.

"I'm going to check out the marathon soon. Getting all of the guys together now. Trying to figure out who is going. You know how it is getting everyone together."

"Oh, I'm jealous," Kelly pouted. "It feels like I'm the only one in Boston who has to work today. It's so nice out! I'm so mad. Maybe next year I could run it!"

"Now that would be cool," JP agreed. "I know you could do it."

Kelly went about her day, doting on the kids, making sure the girl was doing OK, and just trying to keep busy. JP called again. "The guys finally got here. Took forever. Just wanted to say hey. Wish you were here."

"Me, too," she said. "We're watching a bunch of my old movies. It's like a walk down memory lane for me. I gotta take my mind off you guys being out there having fun."

JP laughed. "You're nuts, you know that? But in a good way. I'll give you a call later. Have fun with your movies."

Around 3:15 Kelly got a call from her boss, but they were so engrossed in watching TV she had missed the call. Kelly quickly called back and got her voicemail. "The kids are great, they are both doing fine. We're staying inside and relaxing. I'll talk to you in a bit."

About 10 minutes later she was in the kitchen unloading the dishwashing and her phone rang. Typically if it is an unrecognized number, she lets it go to voicemail, especially while she's working, but for some reason, she answered it this time.

"Hello, is this Kelly?" the disembodied voice asked.

"Yeah." *Who is this*, Kelly thought.

"I'm a social worker at Brigham and Women's Hospital."

"Oh, OK…" Kelly was wracking her brain trying to think of why they were calling her. Is this about a medial assisting job or something to do with school?

"I got your number from JP. He's here. He's been badly hurt. There's been an accident."

What? Kelly's heart sank and her mind started racing. JP was supposed to be leaving the marathon at around 4:00, after Mike J. finished. Now it's only 3:30. Maybe he left early. He must have gotten into a car accident because of all the traffic. Kelly thought to herself. *I've got to keep it together. The kids are in the other room.* Just then she realized she was still holding the phone.

"Uh, OK."

"You need to get here immediately."

"Of course. I'll be right there."

Kelly called her boss. "I've got to leave. JP's been hurt."

"I've got my neighbor coming over right now anyway to take over so you can go."

That was great, but Kelly was a little confused. Why had she already sent the neighbor over? Didn't really matter, she was grateful. The very nice neighbor was there in minutes. "It's OK, I've got the kids. Do you know where you are going?"

"Brigham and Women's Hospital," Kelly told her. The woman just looked at her and Kelly got an odd feeling. The sweet-faced lady was staring at her in silence, as if waiting for Kelly to give more details.

"I can't believe he got into a car accident. I don't know how bad it is. He had better been wearing his seatbelt!" Kelly said as she collected her things.

"Do you know what's going on?" she asked.

"Of course. The marathon," said Kelly. *Strange*, Kelly thought, *everyone knows today is marathon day*. But she was probably concerned that Kelly would have a hard time in traffic. Kelly didn't want to waste any more time trying to figure out what the lady was referring to; she had to get to JP. She was soon off in her car and finally made it to the highway, barreling toward downtown Boston.

"Just get there, just get there," she kept saying to herself. "Just get there. Don't freak out." Kelly knew she could cry at the drop of a hat, so she was determined to keep it together until she found out exactly what had happened. Soon traffic slowed to a crawl and she started to take stock of her surroundings. There seemed to be more sirens than she had ever remembered hearing before. And another thing, the GPS was acting screwy. Something didn't feel right, but she thought it just must be the craziness of the marathon. *And of course*, she thought, *all of this has to happen when JP is in a car accident!*

Suddenly, she got a strange urge, almost a physical tug, to call JP. She hadn't even thought of it before because she was focused on just getting there, and she figured he wouldn't be able to talk anyway if he's hurt. Then she started thinking, *something's not right. Why didn't he call her from the hospital? Why did someone else call her number? They didn't even use his phone. Had he given them her number? He must have.* A tingle crept up her spine like nimble fingers and she felt her cheeks go flush. Suddenly it seemed as if she was floating, looking down at herself in this odd situation, watching to see what her physical self would do. *Is this really happening?*

"Ok, Kelly," she said aloud, "keep it together. You can do this." Then she looked over at the car beside her. There was an attractive young woman, close to her own age, and she was talking on her cell phone and crying hysterically. Kelly started to panic. Something was not right. All of the streets were blocked; traffic wasn't moving; everyone was acting strangely. She pulled over on the side of the road to regroup.

She hadn't spoken to anyone since she had left her babysitting job. Maybe JP's family didn't even know what was going on. She didn't have his mom's number, but she did have Paul's and Jacqui's. She called Paul first and got his voicemail. "JP's been in a really bad accident. Call me as soon as you get this." Next she called Jacqui and left the same message. Since she wasn't able to connect with anyone, she decided to continue on. Just then she got a text from her mother.

HAVE YOU HEARD ABOUT THE EXPLOSION AT THE
MARATHON?

Since she was on the side of the road anyway, she texted back.

No, but JP's been in a bad car accident.
I'm on my way to hospital now.

Kelly eased her car back into the snarled traffic, ready to continue on. Finally the GPS started to work again. Then her phone rang. It was the same woman from the hospital who had called her before.

"Where are you? Is everything OK? Can you get here?"

"I'm on my way. Everything is blocked off."

"Yes, I'm sure it is. I guess you've heard what happened."

"No, I have no idea," she said as she started to cry. She wasn't ready for more news and she knew it wasn't going to be good.

"There's been a really bad explosion."

Then Kelly remembered what her mom had texted to her and started putting it all together. Now it made sense, the thing she didn't want to even consider was exactly what had happened. A word cloud formed in her mind. JP. Marathon. Accident. Explosion. Hospital. It was all connected. "Is he OK?" she asked, not sure if she was ready for the response.

"He's actually in surgery right now."

Kelly knew it was bad. It was real. He was hurt. "What kind of explosion?" she asked.

"I'm not really sure."

Kelly's mind raced again with the tidbits of information she had. Maybe it was a power line explosion or something. Is JP burned? Was there no car accident after all? She hung up the phone and drove on only to get another call. This time it was her father, a military man living in Virginia Beach. Kelly was relieved that he was calling. They have a strong bond and she knew he was the person she needed to hear from right now.

"Are you OK?" He asked.

"Yes, I'm OK, but what is going on, Dad? I haven't seen the news and it's chaos here. I'm driving by myself to go see how JP is and I'm so confused."

"Something horrible happened at the marathon, but they aren't exactly sure what it was. It's all over the news."

"I feel so alone, Dad."

"Kel, I need you to think like a soldier."

"Ok, I can do that."

"I need you to be careful of any people who look strange or out of place. When you get to the hospital, stay away from the edges of the doors, stay away from the trash bins. Just be aware of your surroundings." The tables had turned. That's exactly what Kelly would say to her dad when he had been deployed to various war zones during his military career. It was family looking out for family, but this time he was giving her that advice in her own city. They are not in Iraq. This is Boston. Kelly didn't know what to think, but talking to her dad was a grounding experience and it helped her continue on.

She pulled off at the exit for the hospital, but met up with a roadblock.

"This area is closed," the police officer told her.

"I have to get to the hospital," she said.

"Ma'am do you have someone who was injured at the marathon?"

"Yes," she said, then added for good measure, "my husband." He could see she had been crying—and was still struggling to maintain her composure.

"Go on through."

Kelly felt like she was in an apocalyptic movie as she drove toward the hospital. There were no cars since the roads were blocked. It was as if time stood still. But she knew it wouldn't last as she approached the hospital. She tried to brace herself knowing the next moments would greatly affect her life and the lives of the people she loves. The not knowing was almost unbearable.

She grabbed the bags she had in her car. They contained her laptop, some gym clothes, just a few things she thought she might need at the hospital as she prepared for the unknown. She ran to the main entrance and saw people everywhere. It was like a movie that had been paused and then someone pushed fast-forward. People stared at her as she hurried through. *I must look like shit*, she thought. *Why do I always get so puffy when I cry?* Of course they were watching for relatives and friends of the victims, and she was one of the first to arrive.

Social workers were stopping people as they entered to gather information and try to correlate the visitors with the victims. It was a bizarre triage match game as they tried to get enough clues from the visitor to then identify each John or Jane Doe that now littered the computer system. It was certainly a difficult task when most of the patients had arrived with missing limbs and no identification.

It was a crazy blur, but someone guided Kelly to a family waiting room area to calm her down and get more information.

"What's his name, Miss?"

"Joseph Norden, but he might have said JP," Kelly said, crying like a baby. "Most likely he said JP."

"We're not really sure. He might be in the system as unidentified, but we will figure it out. Take a seat here."

Another woman came over to reassure her that they were looking and would try to find out if JP was there. For a second Kelly worried that it might be the wrong hospital. There are several in a very short radius to this one. That's all she needed was to have to go back on the road. As those thoughts raced through her mind, she looked around the room and took stock of the scene playing out in front of her.

Other families were dealing with similar confusion, asking the same questions, trying to locate loved ones. It was certainly chaotic, but at least she was here and hopefully would get answers soon. Plus, now she wasn't alone. That had been the scary part. Being all alone as the craziness unfolded.

***

Liz's older sister Cheryl was just leaving her shift at the Post Office and driving home with her husband when they heard about the bombing. They were on I-93 and they were worried about a co-worker's daughter who had lost her leg and was running the marathon for Team Spaulding—a team organized by Spaulding Rehabilitation Hospital in Boston.

"I hope she's all right," Cheryl said to her husband as he

dropped her off at the house so he could go get her coffee. Cheryl quickly turned on the TV to see if she could get some news about the marathon. First she called both of her sons—Jimmy who is a mail carrier and, Kevin, a student at Plymouth State. Both said they were fine, so she was able to relax a bit.

As she watched the news about the explosions unfold on TV, her phone started to ring. The caller ID said "Boston Medical" so she quickly answered. She couldn't tell who was on the other end. The person sounded hysterical. She finally figured out it was her sister, Liz.

"Lizzy, what's going on? Where are you?"

"I don't know," Liz said.

"What do you mean you don't know? The phone you're using says Boston Medical. Who are you with?"

"Jonathan."

"Put him on the phone." Cheryl couldn't understand anything Liz was trying to tell her. She was crying uncontrollably.

"I can't," she replied. "He's parking my car."

"What's wrong?"

"Paul's been hurt real bad in the marathon bombing and I don't know where JP is." Then the phone went dead.

Cheryl knew they would have trouble getting into town. She had seen on the news that they were shutting down transfer stations and closing exits. She knew she had to get to her sister so after her husband got home with the coffee, they just started driving toward Boston while she kept trying to get someone else on the phone. Her husband kept asking, "Where are we going?"

"I don't know," Cheryl said. "We just need to get to some hospital." Finally she reached Caitlin. "What's going on?" Cheryl pleaded. "I can't get your mother. Where do I need to go?" She heard her niece crying and trying to speak.

"Caitlin, I can't hear you. We don't know where to go."

A scream like she'd never heard pierced through the phone. "I TOLD YOU BETH ISRAEL WEST!" Then the call was dropped.

Cheryl had never heard Caitlin talk like that. She knew something horrible was happening; she just couldn't exactly figure out what it was. They stopped and asked a transit officer how to get to Beth Israel, since they had never been there.

"You can't go there right now," he told them.

"My nephew is there. I think he was hurt in the marathon bombing."

As they got off at Roxbury, they realized they were in an unfamiliar neighborhood. They weren't sure exactly where they were going, but the officer had given them directions. Cheryl looked out the window and saw a line of cops along the road armed with AK-47s, all in SWAT gear. She started getting nervous. They had to park and walk several blocks to get to the hospital and Cheryl got an eerie feeling. No one seemed to know exactly what was happening, but everyone knew it wasn't good.

They finally reached the hospital and saw familiar faces in the common area. They peered through the window and couldn't believe it. Liz was on the floor crying hysterically. Cheryl was stunned. She wasn't sure what she had expected, but certainly not this. What the hell was happening? She hurried over to comfort her sister.

"Paul's in surgery," Liz said, sobbing. "He's lost a leg. He's real bad. They can't find JP. I think he might be dead."

***

Peter had received almost the exact same phone call as Cheryl. He couldn't tell who was on the phone. It was like time stood still. He knew it wasn't good. Then a male voice came on the line and told him the news: "Uncle Peter we got a call from Paul. He's hurt and we can't find JP." Then silence. Relieved that he had located his wife and his 13-year-old daughter was on her way home, he checked online and began seeing status updates on Facebook.

Did you hear about the bombs?

I was almost going, but didn't.

I can't believe it!

Did you hear about the Norden brothers?

Peter got an uneasy feeling as he saw the messages flooding in. After a few phone calls, he found out that his sister was at Beth Israel. He wasted no time getting over there.

Kelly was waiting in that cramped chair in the family room for a long time, when her phone suddenly rang. It startled her because she hadn't been paying any attention to it before. So lost in thought and worry, she didn't even try to call around. She just set up a vigil and waited and worried and cried. But now someone was calling so she tried to pull herself together. "Hello?" She said, wiping her face.

It was one of their friends from Stoneham. He wanted to know where she was. Did she know where JP was?

"Yes," she said. "I'm at Brigham and Women's."

"His family is looking everywhere for him."

"He's here. I don't have anyone's number. Can you let them know?"

Only a few blocks away at Beth Israel, after getting a phone call about JP, Caitlin and Jonathan hurried over to Brigham and Women's. Their mom was having a hard time dealing with all of this news, especially trying to process the fact that Paul had lost his leg. They decided to see if the information they had was correct. Was JP really there?

At first, the staff wouldn't let them in. All of the hospitals were on high alert and security was tight, but the Nordens were determined. They pleaded to at least be allowed to hang out in the waiting room since, of course, there was no record of a JP Norden in the system. There were lots of people gathered there, but they couldn't find anyone they knew. The word they had gotten was that Kelly was somewhere around here. They just had to find her. They waited until things subsided a bit and went off to search a few other rooms. Finally they found a small family room that was not as crowded as the general waiting area. They scanned the area and saw Kelly curled up on a chair, makeup streaming down her face.

"I didn't know what to do," Kelly told them. "I still haven't gotten any updates about JP. I tried to call Paul and Jacqui, but couldn't get them."

"They are hurt too," Caitlin said.

"Oh my god, you've got to be kidding me. Do you know anything else? I've been so clueless this whole time trying to piece all of this together. Does anybody know what's going on?"

One of the nurses passing by chimed in, "They think it might be terrorists."

Kelly got a sinking feeling, but it made sense. That's why her dad had been so adamant about her safety. Finally, after a long wait, they located a JP Norden in the computer and said he's in surgery.

"The doctor will be calling over here in about 20 minutes," the nurse advised pointing to the wall phone.

Kelly felt relief that he was found, was in surgery, and was apparently alive. Those seemed to be good signs, and she was looking for any good signs she could find at that moment. The young trio sat down and began to wait. Then they got a call that confirmed what Mike had said was true. Paul had lost his leg. As Kelly watched Paul's brother and sister dealing with the news, she just sat in disbelief. What did this mean for JP? What did this mean for all of the Nordens?

Soon another call came in that a close friend of the family also lost one leg and maybe both of them. The three of them sat with their thoughts as this new information sank in. The waiting was excruciating because it seemed like bad news kept pouring in. How much more could this young group of friends handle? And most of all, what was waiting for them from the doctor about JP's condition. For some reason it seemed like everyone's legs were involved, but no one was exactly sure why that was.

"He's going to be OK," Kelly reassured the others. "I know JP is going to be OK. What are the odds that his legs are affected? That would be very unlikely. Let's all stay positive."

"Kelly," Caitlin said, "do you want to sit by the phone since they will be calling soon?" Kelly wasn't sure she was in any shape to handle more news, but she knew that it was necessary. It was important to stay together and stay strong. For Caitlin and Jonathan. For her dad. For JP.

The phone finally rang.

"Hello."

"His injuries are very serious," the doctor began in a friendly but stern tone. "Surgery went really well."

"Oh, good" Kelly said. "Thank you. What a relief."

"His left leg was in really rough shape, but we saved it."

Great, Kelly thought. I told them it would be OK. His leg is fine.

"That leg is looking really good now. Unfortunately we had to amputate his right leg."

As she heard the words, Kelly broke down. She just couldn't believe it. It didn't make sense. How were so many legs affected? And this time it was her boyfriend. It didn't make sense. The phone fell to the ground as Kelly searched her brain for answers. Who would hurt JP? He's the nicest guy around. Ask anyone. It was unimaginable.

As the group sat in silence. Waiting. They all now knew JP was injured like the others. Kelly just wanted to see his face. She just needed to connect with him. Hard to believe she had just left him sleeping this morning. Now that seemed like a lifetime ago. It felt like JP was so far away.

As the hours ticked by in the waiting room, Kelly started to wonder what the future would be like. Is JP going to understand what has happened to him? Is it going to change him? Would their relationship change? There were so many unknowns. That scared Kelly. After three years of dating, they had formed a comfortable rhythm and a familiar routine that now felt damaged beyond repair. How could they return to their previous lives? Being alone with all of those thoughts was difficult, but then she remembered JP was struggling as well and it was up to her to be strong. She was going to get through it, but that didn't mean she wasn't going to cry. Frankly, that was all she could do at that moment. She knew that once she could finally talk to him, things would at least be manageable. They could figure it all out if they were together.

Cheryl and her husband left Liz and Colleen at Beth Israel and walked over to Brigham to see if there had been any news. They quickly spotted Jonathan, Caitlin and another friend in a corner of the family room amongst the huddled, grieving groups dotting the area. Cheryl looked over by the phone and saw a small girl doubled over, hair strewn, and crying violently. *That poor girl,* Cheryl thought. She had only met Kelly once before and didn't recognize her.

Instinctively looking out for her sister, Cheryl found the Family Advocate and called Liz. Liz told them that she had to stay at Beth Israel, but that she gave them permission to give Cheryl, JP's aunt, any medical information and to speak on her behalf. "She's my advocate."

Then Cheryl walked over to her niece and nephew and they took her over to where Kelly was sitting and handed the phone to Cheryl.

"Hello."

"Who am I speaking to?" the doctor asked.

"This is Cheryl, JP Norden's aunt."

"I just want to let you know he came through surgery. He's in real bad shape, but we got him stabilized. As you know, he lost his leg below the knee." Cheryl's steeled herself against the wall, but she kept listening as the doctor listed his many other injuries and the severe burns on his body. We may need to bring an ophthalmologist in to save his eye."

"Oh. OK. Thank you, doctor." Cheryl hung up the phone and told her husband what she'd heard. "We can't call Lizzy and tell her this. We've got to go over there." On the way back to the other hospital Cheryl couldn't believe she was going to have to tell her sister that her other son had lost his leg too. Knowing that her sister gets nervous and really doesn't have anyone to lean on besides her children, Cheryl knew she couldn't cry. It would be too much for Liz to take.

Cheryl broke the news as best she could and saw her sister fall apart all over again. She knew she had to stay strong for Lizzy because she could see the fear and desperation in her face. Liz didn't know which hospital to stay at or what to do. Her capacity for bad news about her own children was overflowing. It was more than any mother should have to endure.

After hearing about her brother's leg, Caitlin had to sit down. This information overload was a lot of handle. She felt like she was going to faint. "I just need to be alone," she told Jonathan. She found a somewhat secluded area of the waiting room and decided to stay there for a while to gather her composure. A social worker came over to her, put her hands on Caitlin and said, "Relax. It's all right. I'm breathing for you. Concentrate on my breathing. Each breath is a bridge to another breath."

As family and friends huddled in the waiting room at Beth Israel, they saw teams of officers with ATF printed in large letters on their jackets. They were told that everyone should stay where they are because they would need to be questioned. No one should enter or leave until their investigation was complete.

They began assembling families in small groups to question them and find out if they had any information, if they had seen anything that might help the investigation. Liz was of little use because she was so distraught that focusing on these questions was just not going to happen.

It was the last day for one of the chaplains at Beth Israel. She was going to work at another hospital and her shift was over, but she wouldn't leave. She told Liz that she was going to stay with her and her family for as long as necessary.

It was the beginning of what would be an odyssey of medical jargon, decision-making, and the mass influx of friends, family, and complete strangers offering their support, prayers, and anything else the Nordens needed.

They still had not seen either JP or Paul yet, but at least both had been located and they were both alive—something Liz hadn't been sure of just a few minutes before. As they tried to handle the overload of emotions and the massive mental strain of the situation, it was inspiring to those watching from the sidelines. This family was pulling together, circling the wagons, and fielding calls from concerned friends, neighbors, and coworkers.

***

The doting, indefatigable chaplain who insisted on staying with them was a mere hint of the massive outpouring of support and community spirit that would wash over them in the days, weeks, and months to come. This working-class family isn't famous or rich or privileged. They are just regular people who try to earn the best living they can as they enjoy the quaint town of Stoneham and the rowdy, contagious spirit of nearby Boston. It's all that they really know and they like it that way.

Being together has always been the most important part of their day—it certainly isn't the work and it isn't the promise of a sparkling future off in the distance. They all live for the moment and enjoy each minute. They had begun to spread out a bit with JP out on his own and Paul likely to follow soon, but everyone still felt the most comfortable and the most content when they all got together at Liz's house to eat, hang out, and give each other a hard time.

What this unsuspecting and unassuming family didn't realize was that they had an amazing network of people—many they knew, but most they did not—who would offer to do whatever they could to help ease the devastating effects of the horrible, unsuspecting tragedy that had Boston in its grip with no sign of letting go.

They huddled together, worrying their way through that first night, sharing with each other any piece of information they received and offering to make trips to get each other food, drinks—anything, everything. As this scared family clung to any news they could get, and as they watched the hours tick away until they could actually see their fallen—they may not have realized it but their bonds grew stronger. That strength was all they had to get them to the next day.

***

Kevin Casey, a senior at Plymouth State, about 100 miles from Stoneham, was in his dorm room when his mom called to tell him about his cousins. He found out that Paul had lost his leg, but he was still in disbelief. Cheryl told her son that JP also lost his leg and Paul was not doing well at all. Kevin wasted no time in packing his bags, borrowing his roommate's car, and driving straight home. That first night he and his mom stayed up late, mesmerized by the news of the marathon on TV. It seemed like the news and images continued to wash over them, nonstop, coating them with layer upon layer of information about the unimaginable tragedy that had fallen upon their city of Boston. *Paul can't die*, Kevin thought. *What would I do without him and JP?*

They hurried into Boston early the next morning, with little sleep and even less hope, as Kevin reunited with his cousins Jonathan, Caitlin, Colleen, friend Mike J. and all of the others holding vigil. It was comforting for Kevin to be close to everyone instead of off at school, but the only thing they could do was wait and keep each other company.

On April 19, as they continued their vigil in the Beth Israel waiting room, Caitlin saw a flurry of activity outside. She got everyone's attention and Liz, Kevin and Cheryl were mesmerized as about fifteen police cruisers and three ambulances pulled up to the emergency room entrance.

They all watched in shock as the officers rushed past them holding either side of someone covered with a blanket. They looked up at the TV in the waiting room and saw that a suspect had been apprehended in the marathon bombing case. According to the news he was being taken to a place in Cambridge, but they turned and saw the same TV image playing out in front of them.

Maybe the information reported was to keep the true location confidential because of the already enraged community, and the use of three ambulances was likely to provide decoys if needed because all eyes were on Boston around the clock—every move scrutinized.

Liz wasted no time addressing the nurse on duty. "I do not want anyone who deals with him to come in contact with my son! I can't believe they brought him here!"

"We had no idea they were coming here," the nurse explained as she apologized. "They will be kept on a different floor, with a different staff. I'll make sure of it."

Whether or not that was true, the family felt a slight bit of comfort in that information. Liz had purposely been avoiding the news because she wanted to focus all of her energy on her sons. She was aware that a manhunt had been underway for the last few days, and of course she heard bits and pieces, but she made a conscious effort to keep thinking in a positive direction. Until her sons were conscious, she didn't have time to devote to anything else.

The people who had perpetrated such an act, whether it was this guy or someone else, they had not just attacked random people at a marathon—they had attacked her family. She was not about to give them any of her time or attention. They didn't deserve it.

All she wanted was for her sons to regain consciousness.

***

Siobhan Cooper, an RN in the trauma ICU at Beth Israel, had just returned from attending a wedding in Hawaii with her husband.

They had arrived at their apartment near Fenway at around 2:30. Just as they settled down to rest for a few minutes, both of their cell phones starting going off. They hadn't even had the TV on; they had just been so tired from the red-eye flight.

Friends and family kept asking if they were OK. Someone said to turn on the TV. Siobhan's husband is a critical care fellow and anesthesiologist, so both being in the medical profession they knew what they had to do. They each got ready quickly and raced out of the door since they were so close to the hospital. They hurried to Beth Israel and were awestruck by the controlled chaos. Siobhan stopped in her tracks for a moment and proudly watched the coordinated precision of the staff. Not only were medical personnel working long shifts, but hoards of volunteers had shown up to selflessly devote themselves to helping with the influx of patients.

Siobhan sprang into action, assisting in the trauma ICU which is used as the ER recovery unit. The scene reminded her of a MASH center in a war zone with all of the sights and sounds, but also because of the relatively young age of most of the victims— an unfortunate reality during wartime. Most of the patients were the same—covered in soot with a strong smell of burning hair, ash, and flesh. She immediately started working feverishly on one of the patients when she noticed his wedding ring. She wanted to remove it and save it for him because when it came time for surgery, she thought that would be something he'd regret if it got lost. It was stuck, but with a little lubrication, she was able to slip it off. She looked at the inscription inside and noticed the wedding date which was only a week before her own. It hit her that this could have been her, her husband or any of their friends lying here.

She immediately felt an intense and genuine connection with her new patients.

After about an hour on duty, she was treating a white male who had just come from the operating room. He was covered in soot like the others, eyebrows burned off, and his right leg amputated. He was unstable and still bleeping profusely from the stump, the trauma area. She knew the surgeries were being performed quickly to first save lives, and then they could go back and concentrate on the aesthetics.

As she worked on getting him stable, she saw the array of tattoos on his body—an inky story she didn't yet understand. He had been identified only in the briefest of terms: male, approximately 52 years old. *OK*, she thought, *this is a pretty cool 52-year-old we have here with all of this ink*. She continued with her work, cleaning his face, getting him stable, and redressing the stump area. He was obviously a strong guy, a fighter. It was about 8:30 that night so as she prepared to leave for the day, she ran into the family in the hallway and was immediately impressed.

"That's my son, Paul," Liz told her. "He's 31, he'll be 32 in a couple of months."

Ah, that made more sense. Siohban had thought he seemed much younger, especially after she had cleaned him off, but at first, it was certainly difficult to tell.

The next morning, she saw that the family was still there, still vigilant. As she talked with them, she was amazed by their loyalty and dedication to each other. It was obvious and immediate. Unfortunately, she saw far too many patients who had little or no support system, at a time when it's most critical. To see the Nordens and their steely resolve was truly refreshing. The waiting area was still on lockdown and still in chaos, with intimidating armed guards monitoring every door using high-tech radios and determined expressions.

As the days wore on, she became Paul's primary nurse. Anytime she was on duty, she was assigned to him and of course his family. She felt an immediate kinship with her patient even though he was in a comatose state. It didn't matter. She had learned so much about him from his family that she knew he was someone she'd like to know. It was also helpful to get some background information on him because once she learned that he's a more reserved, private type of person, she knew to keep that in mind when she could finally talk to him. She had learned to quickly assess a patient's personality type in order to know how to best communicate.

While continuing to administer care, she couldn't help but notice the droves of family and friends that flowed into and out of the hospital each and every day. Someone was always around so that Paul was never alone, not for a minute. It was amazing to see that kind of dedication at a level she had never witnessed before.

She knew this support was going to be crucial for Paul in the weeks, months, and even years ahead. He has a lot of challenges in front of him. There will be many ups and downs as he learns to adjust to a new normal, a life as an amputee. But with this family behind him, he has a big advantage over many of the patients she sees.

CHAPTER 6 – VIGILS

As she was rushed into the emergency entrance at Tufts, Jacqui saw medical staff lining the hallways, waiting for arrivals. She heard someone say, "Here's the first one" as they hurried her into the emergency room to what seemed like an endless supply of doctors and nurses coming in and questioning her. She was understandably confused and overwhelmed as she was rushed into surgery.

At the same time, there was a detective asking her questions about the event and what she remembered, but she wasn't much help. It was mass confusion. Her friends had been hanging out together and the next thing they know, they're carelessly tossed along Boylston Street. She was glad to at least be in the hospital, but with the pain and the barrage of questions, she felt small and alone.

Soon a doctor hurried into the room, still in his running gear, obviously straight from the marathon. Jacqui watched as he surveyed the room and asked if everything was under control. After being satisfied that all of these patients were being cared for, he was off again, announcing that he was going to check on the others that had been arriving to the hospital at a steady clip. As she was being wheeled into the operating room, she kept asking one question even though she was terrified of what the response might be. "Will I lose my leg? Can you tell me? I know it's bad. Just tell me. Will I lose my leg?"

Most of staff that she asked avoided the question. On a rational level she understood. They had to assess the damage and go from there. She got that, but she also knew what she had seen on that bloody street. She could easily meet the same fate. Finally, to her relief, one of the doctors spoke up. "No. Your legs are very badly damaged, but we are going to save them."

A nurse came over to Jacqui to help her. "Let me get you cleaned up a little," she said. Jacqui's face was hidden by the black soot that covered her body, and her hair was singed and pungent. Several areas of her skin would remain blackened for weeks before it would begin to slowly subside.

"Can you call my mom?" Jacqui asked the nurse.

A voice came from across the room. "I don't think we can make calls yet because of what's going on in the city."

The nurse left the room and quickly returned with her personal cell phone. "Don't worry," she said. "Let's call your mom now." The nurse calmly advised Jacqui's mom to head to Tufts, not Boston Medical as previously indicated. Jacqui was relieved that soon she would be able to connect with her family after the ordeal she had endured. "Let's finish cleaning you up before your mom gets here."

Next she was wheeled into the x-ray room to get a CAT scan. "Can I get a hair elastic," Jacqui asked one of the radiologists.

"Oh, don't worry about your hair," she said.

"I'm not worried. It's in my face and the smell is making me sick."

"Oh, of course, let me fix it!" She put it up in a bun that would remain in place for the next five days.

Finally, on the way out of the x-ray room, Jacqui saw her mother, her twin sister and her aunt. Relief swept over her as she got to see her family. It helped her feel a little better despite the intense pain. Jacqui turned to her sister, "People lost limbs and I think JP lost his leg. You need to call them to find out if they're OK.

"Of course," she said. "I'll take care of it."

She felt some small amount of comfort that her family was nearby as she was wheeled into surgery and soon lost consciousness. Later, Jacqui woke up in ICU with intense pain. She saw her hands bandaged and could feel the burning in one of them. Shrapnel had been partially removed from the other and the wounds had been tightly dressed. It was later that night when Jacqui was recovering and finally taking stock of what had actually occurred. Her family was in the room and she quickly asked her sister for clarification.

"Did JP really lose his leg? It's all such a blur."

"Yes," she said solemnly.

"How's Paul?"

"He's in recovery."

Despite the fact that her hearing was still severely compromised, she got the gist of what everyone was saying. She tried to process the information, but that first night was filled with anxiety, frustration, and severe pain. She couldn't sleep, couldn't get comfortable, and couldn't stop thinking about how the others were doing—especially Paul.

Still partially in shock, Jacqui was in the darkened room with vacuum packs on her legs to help with the wounds. For some reason, the pressurized bags kept bursting and panic overtook her as the staccato pops punctured the still air. It was much too reminiscent of what she had experienced that afternoon. Throughout that night, she wasn't allowed to eat or drink because more surgery was planned for the next morning. Every three hours they would bring medication for her to take, but without food, she got sick each time. All she wanted was a glass of water, but she couldn't have it.

Her hearing made it seem as if cotton balls had been stuffed into her ears. She couldn't tell where noises were coming from. Because both eardrums were perforated, her hearing was malfunctioning and it was disorienting, eerily quiet, and unimaginably scary. After some experimentation, she found that if she laid on her left side with her right ear in the pillow, it was at least tolerable.

On her second day in the hospital, her mom gave her the distressing news. "I'm afraid I have some news about Paul that you need to hear."

"What do you mean?" Jacqui asked. "Did you get an update?"

"Something like that. You need to know that he lost his right leg." She was very direct and to the point.

"Are you sure? I—I don't know what to say. None of this seems real." Still in shock, three things went through her mind and they were all about him: he loves to play basketball, he loves to walk his dogs, and he loves his sneaker collection. Those things were so much a part of his life that she wondered what the future would hold for him—for both of them.

***

That Monday night, the senseless tragedy still fresh in her mind, Liz left at around 2:30 to go home, change clothes, and take care of Paul's dogs. Sure, she could have asked one of the many willing supporters to help with that, but she wanted to do it herself. Both of her sons were in comas so there was nothing she could do at the hospitals. This way she felt useful and she felt like she was somehow connecting with them by taking care of these routine tasks.

She knew that both of her sons were in good hands. Caitlin, Jonathan and Mike decided to stay with Paul to make sure he was never alone. Kelly set up camp by JP's side with family members coming in and out hoping for any update, and glimmer of hope that either would soon awaken.

When JP finally came out of his first round of emergency surgeries, the nurse told JP's father and Kelly that he was not conscious, but they could see him. JP was sedated with tubes and wires snaking unnaturally out of his body. He didn't look like himself. He was so banged up and covered with soot and burns and injuries that while Kelly knew it was him, she had an odd sensation, like this was an impostor. She held his hand to at least try to establish a connection. She was so glad to finally lay her eyes on him. She began to take stock. His hair was burned, his eyebrows completely seared off. His eyelashes were singed to a crisp. His hands covered in the ever-present black soot. It was a lot to comprehend all at once. It had been such a great morning. How could it ended up like this? It was so hard to believe.

Having a strong stomach, she knew she could handle whatever she saw. She lifted up the sheet to assess his legs. Seeing that one was missing below the knee was just so surreal. She had just left him this morning, rubbing his legs as she said goodbye like she always did. He had been so happy, and he had been excited to hang out with his brother and pals to watch Mike run. How could such a genuinely nice guy go from that to lying in a hospital bed with permanent, life-altering injuries?

JP was obviously heavily sedated, but Kelly kept holding and rubbing his hands to warm him, to generate some kind of a connection. She had the urge to clean him up and try to make him feel better. She wanted a lot of things, but mostly she just wanted to talk to him. All she could do was hope for the best as tears traveled down her cheeks.

There was still a lot of activity with the nurses and doctors tending to JP the first night so Kelly opted to stay out in the waiting room. She didn't want to be in the way during this critical time of recovery. By now the waiting room was packed with people, most of them finally getting information and slowly processing the grim, harsh reality of the situation. Lots of JP's friends and family were starting to gather and Kelly greeted them and gave a brief update on his progress.

That night Kelly woke up to find herself curled up in a chair, underneath a blanket, eyes crusted over from crying in her sleep. She went into the bathroom and saw that her face was puffy, makeup a disaster, and salt caked around her eyes. There were even clumps in her eyelashes, her hair, it was everywhere.

The next day found the Norden brothers, Jacqui, and surely many other victims in the throes of life-saving surgery. Teams of medical personnel worked tirelessly to do as much as possible to address the trauma areas and save their lives. The primary concern was to stop the bleeding and address the missing limbs. Paul and JP were in ICU, both on breathing tubes, and both in comas.

Mike Jefferson arrived at Beth Israel to find an atmosphere of uncertainty. At first, no one seemed to know what was going on. He was desperate to get information on his friends—the guys who had come to support him as he ran the marathon. When he first got to see Paul, he was unconscious and looked almost unrecognizable. Mike couldn't believe what had happened to these guys—he was close with JP, Paul and Jonathan and seeing them hurting, all in different ways, was hurting him too.

Later he made his way over to Brigham and saw JP, also unconscious and swollen beyond belief. Mike went back to Beth Israel to stay there for the night. He told the nurse on duty, "If anything changes, wake me up." That night he holed up in a small waiting area only to find himself disoriented when he woke up. Why was he here? Then it came back to him. The marathon. Bombing. JP. Paul.

There's not anything he wouldn't do for these guys, so he found a small bench in the hallway outside of Paul's room. He knew that Kelly and the others were watching over JP, so he decided to keep Jonathan company and stay with Paul as long as it took. He found that at 5'8" he fit just fine on that bench and it would become his home away from home for almost a month.

Friends and family poured into and out of each hospital offering up help and any kind of assistance possible. Several of Stoneham's own were fighting for their lives, and the small town wasted no time rallying to their aid. Lots of people contacted the Nordens to see how they could help. Many visited to show support, and others even began talk of coordinating fund-raising efforts for the unavoidable bills that would be piling up.

Because of its configuration, the family found that Beth Israel accommodated the ever-growing crowd a bit easier than Brigham. It didn't really matter since it was a quick walk between the two. Liz was flabbergasted by the sheer numbers of people calling, texting, and dropping by. And just because she wasn't at her house, that didn't change her natural inclination to make everyone feel welcomed. In between dealing with medical decision-making, she made sure to thank each person for coming, ensured that they were comfortable, and basically created an extension of her own home. The staff at both hospitals commented that they had never seen so many friends and supporters for any of their patients. While it was truly inspiring, Liz wasn't surprised by it. She knew that all of her kids have lots of friends and with their long-standing ties in the area, most everyone either knows the Nordens or at least knows of them.

Along the hospital corridors, just below the "No Food Allowed" sign, cases of soda, water, and snacks magically appeared and lined the walls, being restocked as soon as they were emptied. The staff turned a blind eye to the typically enforced rules due to the extenuating circumstances. This event had affected the entire city and consequently the world. They realized that the support of these struggling patients was crucial to their recovery. At any given time, the waiting room was littered with sleeping bags, blankets, and pillows as people curled up for fits of sleep between the bursts of patient updates. The loyalty was undeniable.

Kelly made a conscious decision to approach the next day with renewed hope. Maybe JP would be able to talk. Until then she decided she would just be a fly on the wall, not leaving until they ran her out. Even though the Nordens were there too, she did want to miss any of the constant updates about JP. She filled the time talking to herself and talking to him as if he could hear her, because maybe he could.

That night the medical staff came into JP's room and gave the family some great news. They were going to take him off the respirator, ease off on the sedation, and try to wake him up. The family gathered around and Kelly held his hand as they reduced the dosage of medicine. They yelled loudly knowing that his hearing was likely affected from the blasts.

"JP, JP, wake up! It's time to wake up. You're at the hospital." To no avail.

"Why don't you give it a try," the nurse told Kelly.

"OK." Kelly readied herself beside him and began squeezing his hand and letting go, and squeezing again, hoping that might help bring him around. "JP, it's Kelly, please wake up. I need to see your eyes. I haven't seen your eyes. I need to see them. Please wake up!" As his eyes fluttered Kelly held the bed for balance. It was as if the wind was knocked out of her tiny body. She couldn't believe he might actually see her again.

"You're at the hospital. Do you know what happened?"

He moaned, but didn't really respond. "JP, you have to open your eyes. Just look at me."

And he did.

It was brief, but Kelly had seen his brown eyes, the eyes she had looked into every night for the last three years. They were just as she had remembered. The medical team worked to remove the tube from his throat. He had been pulling at it off and on, but now it was finally out. He was breathing on his own. He opened his eyes again and focused on Kelly.

"You don't have to yell," he told her. "Just talk loud."

Kelly smiled. "Do you know what happened?" she asked.

"Yeah," he said. "My leg."

"Yeah," Kelly said as she started crying again. She almost felt like it would never end.

"Who does this to someone?" JP whispered.

"I don't know," was all she could say. "I don't know."

After a few minutes, Kelly was back in command. "We'll get through it. Don't worry about that."

JP looked at her. "You don't deserve this."

"Oh stop it," Kelly said trying to lighten the mood. "I deserve you and I'll take you any which way." He responded with the smirk she knew so well. "We're going to get through it," she said. "This is a huge bump in the road, but we can get through anything. We deserve each other. It will be fine."

Kevin looked at his cousin—the man he had always looked up to, whose advice he'd always sought—who was now almost unrecognizable. It was tough to see JP in that condition so he tried to be nonchalant. He didn't want to see alarmed. Then he looked down and saw the bandaged stump resting on a pillow as the other leg continued on to the end of the bed—a permanent reminder of that tragic Monday.

As Kevin regained his composure, JP looked around the room at his mom and the rest of his family. He also saw that a few of his buddies were gathered in the small room.

"Hey," JP said pointing to one of his friends. "I was supposed to drive you to the airport for your vacation. Do you still need a ride?"

They laughed and assured him that all he needed to focus on was getting better. As Caitlin tried to get his attention, JP pretended he couldn't hear her. "What's that noise?" he said. She smiled.

He was back.

With all of the medical information being hurled at Liz over the next several days, she was so glad to have family to rely on. Her siblings—especially Peter and Cheryl—were determined to help her navigate the maze of medical decisions and jargon that she was getting from each hospital. "Cheryl was so helpful," Liz told everyone. "It is difficult with so much medical information coming from both directions. Sometimes there is disappointing news about one son and good news about the other—and then it would switch. It is just a lot to process. Having Cheryl's direct approach and Peter's affable personality is the only way I can handle everything that is happening and keep my sanity."

As Paul continued to fight for his life, JP dealt with the passing days by thinking about what had happened and trying to sort out what his future would be like. After crying a lot as he dealt with painful surgeries, burn treatments, and shrapnel removal, he drew strength from thinking back to the day his body was pummeled with metal and his leg ripped from his body. He was proud of how he and his brother had helped Jacqui and looked out for each other. He knew they had just gone into survival mode. When he saw that he was missing a leg, it didn't seemed like such a big deal at the time. At least he was alive and he could see that his brother was going through a very similar experience. He was more concerned for everyone else.

They had told him that when he arrived at the hospital, he would have been lucky to have about a liter of blood left in his system. He had suffered such a great amount of blood loss that it was amazing he was conscious and alert. While he knew about his right leg, he hadn't realized how damaged the left was. He had come close to losing that one as well and he still faced weeks of surprise infections and other setbacks as he fought to heal and go home. He also knew he was have to endure more of the vacuum-assisted closure (VAC) devices used to create a seal over the wound and promote healing, but he found them uncomfortable and noisy.

Liz was so glad to have one of her sons conscious and talking and communicative. She was amazed at his strength and how he was handling his injuries. She assured him that he was going to be all right and he could come stay with her when he got out. She would naturally dedicate herself to helping him as much as she could. He knew that, but was also glad to hear it.

During that time, Liz struggled with just how much information to give him about his brother, and naturally JP kept asking about Paul, Jacqui and his other friends. With Paul still in a coma, she didn't want to alarm him so while he kept asking questions, she would distract him.

"Why can't Paul call me? When can I see him?"

"He's in surgery," she would say or "He's sleeping right now."

She felt incredibly guilty because she had always prided herself on being straight-forward and direct with her children, never holding back. Now she felt like it was the best thing to do. There was nothing JP could do right now, so it was best if he just focused on himself, but the bond that he and Paul share is strong, and he likely realized that she was trying to protect him. She worried that if something fatal happened to Paul, would JP understand? It bothered her, but she had to stay strong and stick with her conviction.

The community was glued to their respective TV sets as they watched the news updates about the devastating tragedy that had struck their city. And each night there would be a list of the number of critical patients at each hospital in the Boston area. To everyone's relief, as each day passed, the number of people in critical care would decrease. By the middle of the first week, there was only one patient still listed in critical condition each night on the news, only one patient still in a coma. That patient was at Beth Israel. That patient was Paul Norden.

Initially, Paul's right leg was amputated just below the knee, but the knee was badly damaged and on Thursday night of the first week, the decision was made to go in through the knee and re-amputate above to generate enough skin to create an effective stump. Liz understood and agreed with the doctor's recommendation. As she, Cheryl, and the rest of the family waited for results of the surgery, they got the report that his fever had spiked and he was turning septic—which meant an infection was compromising his immune system. The family was tense and anxious, but all they could do was wait it out and hope he pulled through.

They weren't sure what was causing the sudden change in his condition. He had suffered multiple third-degree burns, especially a particularly serious one on his arm, and those are notoriously susceptible to infection. His fever continued to climb first to 102 then up to 104. The doctors were conducting tests and trying everything, but they were unsure of the exact cause and hesitated to predict an outcome.

President and Mrs. Obama were attending a service at the Cathedral of the Holy Cross and a nurse suggested that Liz go since there was nothing to do but wait. Liz was a nervous wreck, but at this point all she could do was pray that JP would keep getting better, and hope that Paul would pull through despite these recent complications. She prayed in the name of her mother (who they called Sal) that her son would pull through. Paul and Sal were very close, so Liz decided it couldn't hurt to channel her energy into prayer and healing. Everyone was just hoping to get some good news about Paul the next day. Cheryl prepared to head home and get some rest while other family members stayed at the hospital. But before she left, Cheryl told the doctor, "Please call me if anything serious happens. Liz has enough to deal with right now. Let me know and I'll tell her."

At 11:46 p.m. her bedside phone rang, violently piercing the gentle silence, causing Cheryl to sit upright, heart pounding wildly. *Oh no!* Cheryl thought this has to be about Paul and they were only going to call if it was an emergency. How much more could this family handle? Her husband answered and then handed her the phone. *It's Peter.*

She felt a wave of relief. Her brother was calling to tell her about the latest news of the manhunt going on in Boston. At first, Cheryl couldn't even focus on his words. She was just so glad the call wasn't about Paul. She thought for sure that he wasn't going to make it through the night by the way he looked when she had left the hospital. She had never been so glad to hear Peter's voice.

Fortunately, on Friday they got news that Paul's fever had broken. They had located the infection area and successfully treated it. They were still concerned about the potential for pneumonia and, even though he was sustained in a coma by various drugs including Propofol, whenever they had to suction out fluid, his eyes would pop open and then close again. While in the coma, he would occasionally raise his arms at random times and seemingly he was trying to open his eyes—while it was a little startling, these actions gave the family hope that soon he would awaken.

On Saturday, almost a week after he had been brought in, when their hope had begun to wane and doubt set in, his medications were reduced and Paul finally woke up. He had remembered calling his mom on the phone as he had been loaded into the ambulance and he remembered the dedicated EMTs who helped save his life. Then he felt something odd on his face and realized there was a tube going down his throat. The choking sensation was too much to handle.

"I saw Jonathan when I opened my eyes," he said, "and I started to cry because I was so happy to see him. During the coma I could hear them talking, hear the voices. I remember hearing Caitlin, Jonathan, Mike, and Kevin a lot, and I wondered why I couldn't wake up. I wanted to open my eyes and tell them I was here, but I couldn't. I felt trapped, but there was nothing I could do. I also kept seeing a black sign with a red X. I don't know what it meant, but somehow it related to what happened to me that day."

Liz had been ecstatic when she got the call to come to the hospital because Paul had removed his breathing tube. Someone was going to come by and pick her up, but she couldn't wait. She called a cab and rushed back to the place she had been every day for the last week. Just seeing him awake was the best day of her life because it meant both of her sons were alive. That was something she wasn't sure of only a few days before.

Kevin had to excuse himself and spend some time in the hallway. After seeing Cousin Paul's still body finally come to life, it was a lot to handle. He needed some time to pull himself together and process this emotional week. Bonding with his cousins during their vigil had been helpful for everyone, but finally seeing Paul's eyes was a moment he'd never forget.

Having spent so much time looking at her brother's swollen face and bandaged limbs, Caitlin had been afraid he wouldn't make it. She knew her brother was strong, but with each passing day in a coma, she feared the worst. It was tough for her and Colleen to see their brothers like this. Colleen thought back to growing up with them, how they were the authority figures in the house as Mom was out working. She remembered how supportive they had been when she got pregnant. *Whatever you decide to do, we're here for you,* they had both told her. That was important because, of course, she wanted their support and approval.

Still with a breathing tube in his throat, and obviously a bit groggy and disoriented, they could all see by his expression that he was glad to finally be able to see everyone. He kept motioning to the tube, but they assured him that it would be taken out soon. The nurses had promised him that it could come out the next day at midnight and he was focused on that. It was obviously uncomfortable and he was frustrated because he couldn't talk. Jonathan was in the room talking and just trying to keep Paul distracted when he kept raising his hand. Jonathan wasn't sure what he was trying to tell them, but he kept holding up his fingers, first three, then two and then one. He was watching the clock and counting down until the tube could come out, and then he yanked on it, removing it himself instead of waiting for the nurse. His voice was horse and scratchy, but he could finally talk with his family and friends. It was an important step because that meant the number of critical patients went down to zero.

Paul asked Mike J. to come in and they got to talk for a while. Then he asked about Jacqui and JP. He gave Jacqui a call, but she didn't answer since it was late. The next day Paul was inundated with people who wanted to talk to him. They had all watched him struggle for the past week and finally they could actually communicate with him. It was an important breakthrough. He also was able to finally talk to Jacqui for the first time. He had been updated on her condition, but he was relieved to hear her voice. Next they arranged so he could FaceTime with JP, the brother he hadn't talked to in a week, since that fateful Monday. Since they had not told him anything, Paul told his brother that he had lost his leg. Of course, JP knew that, but he also broke the news to Paul that he had lost his leg also. "It will be OK," Paul told him, "maybe Oprah will buy you a house or something." JP laughed as he realized his brother was still groggy from the medications, but at least they had connected. Hopefully soon they could see each other.

To combat the scratchy throat brought on by the breathing tube, Paul became obsessed with cherry popsicles, asking for them constantly. His nurse, Siobhan, kept telling him that he had reached his limit for the day and couldn't have any more, but then she would give in. If they made him this happy, it's worth it, she reasoned.

As Jacqui was recuperating at Tufts, she was anxious for the day when she could talk to Paul. She noticed that he had tried to call her at around 2 a.m. one night, but she had been asleep. He had also called her sister, but didn't leave a message. That meant that he was awake! She was so excited. Then at 6:00 the next morning her phone rang. He was groggy but awake and eager to finally talk to the girlfriend who had been torn from his grip on Boylston Street. Jacqui wanted to tell him so many things, but she tempered that urge for now. It would be better when they were together.

When she finally got to see Paul in person, it was a welcome relief and a challenge at the same time. As a couple, they were forced to wrestle with the realities of their altered physical states. Their conversations were intimate, difficult, and intense. As each regained a bit more mobility, they were able to examine their relationship and what it would mean going forward…if they chose to continue together.

"You don't have to stay with me. You know that, right? I'm banged up. I've only got this one leg now," Paul said solemnly. He couldn't imagine being a burden to anyone.

Jacqui was so happy to hear his voice, but couldn't believe what he was saying. It broke her heart. She certainly understood his position. He's a proud man with a new set of circumstances that he had to deal with.

"It's gonna be a wheelchair for me. You don't want that and I don't want that for you."

"Paul—"

"No, Jacqui, I'm serious. I can't even work. How am I gonna work? How are we supposed to have a life together? Forget about it."

She felt horrible that Paul was having to think about this while dealing with his injuries. It was important that they spend one-on-one time together to figure things out, but the two hospitals couldn't coordinate a visit between both of their surgery schedules and the sheer bureaucracy of allowing her out of the hospital temporarily.

Finally, Jacqui couldn't wait any longer and was able to negotiate a reprieve where they would allow her to check out of the hospital for a couple of days and be readmitted again. That way she would have a little bit of time to face Paul directly and let him know that she was in love with him, regardless of his leg.

Jacqui was so nervous leading up to that meeting. It would be a pivotal time for their relationship and the rest of her life. If he was adamant about his feelings, there was nothing she could do to change that. She just hoped she could reason with him.

Since she was restricted to a wheelchair, her sister guided her into the hospital to meet with Paul. She had butterflies in her stomach. This man she had spent the last few years with, and who made her feel more at ease than anyone on earth, was now making her apprehensive. Despite the pain, she had to push that aside; she knew it was time to talk.

She braced herself for a difficult conversation, one that she had replayed many times in her head, but when she saw him, it was as if they had never been apart. Being separated was the difficulty; that's what had allowed doubt to creep in. When they saw each other, they both realized that. She could see in his eyes that he was so happy that she was there. He knew the effort it must have taken for her to get to him and she had done it. They both knew at that moment that they were going to see each other through this. This wasn't the end of them. It was just a part of their ongoing journey together.

Over the next days and weeks, they would visit each other as often as they could and of course they talked on the phone constantly. They were never going to let their connection be broken again.

***

As Paul and JP continued to focus on their recovery, they talked to each other daily on the phone, waiting until they could finally see each other. Until then, they began getting visitors from the outside world as the nation came to grips with what had happened in Boston on April 15.

In the earlier days, Michelle Obama came by to see JP, but he was in and out of consciousness and wouldn't remember much of the visit. It would have been great to say hi to the First Lady, but his health came first. That was the only challenge with famous visitors calling on the brothers. Their intentions were not only admirable, they were much appreciated; however, with that kind of trauma, good days and bad days are inevitable. They never knew how they would feel from one day to the next. It would just depend on the success of the most recent surgery.

The cast of the reality show *Wicked Tuna* also came through Brigham and Women's and tried to pay JP a visit, but again he was not up to receiving guests. Granted everyone understood due to the tough situation. Actor Kevin Spacey even dropped by and cheered everyone up. He was so down to earth that they couldn't believe this busy man took time out of his schedule to come visit them.

Spacey had been filming in New York when he heard about the tragedy and decided to pay a visit to Beth Israel. He saw Paul and his family, putting a smile on everyone's face in the room.

"Hey, you're the negotiator," Paul said recalling his role as a police negotiator.

"You were a hell of a negotiator!" Pete chimed in. "I'm Peter Brown."

"Oh, Uncle Pete, right," Spacey said as he posed for pictures and signed autographs, trying to keep a low profile, just hoping to make a difference.

"Maybe I could take a role in your next movie," Uncle Peter offered, to no one's surprise.

"You'd take up the whole fuckin' camera," Spacey said.

Besides the influx of visitors, everyone at the hospital had to cope with the throngs of media people searching for information and trying to find story angles. The Nordens became in-demand topics for news features and articles. Early on during their hospital stay, Caitlin was interviewed by Anderson Cooper on CNN. She talked about how severe both of her brothers' injuries were, in addition to the fact that they had each lost a leg.

New England Patriots cornerback, Devin McCourty, had seen the interview, found her on Facebook and sent her a message saying that he was thinking of the family. She quickly thanked him and he asked if he could send them something. In a few days a very generous gift basket arrived for the brothers. Caitlin also mentioned that while JP was a fan of the team, Paul loves the Baltimore Ravens, and especially cornerback Ray Rice.

In no time, Caitlin had a video message on her phone that she played for Paul after he woke up. It was his favorite ball player,

Ray Rice, telling him to stay tough and get better. When he saw it, Paul couldn't believe it. "This is amazing! I'm nobody and he's a superstar and he sent me a message." He also invited them to come to a game when they felt better.

All of those visits and well-wishes were great, but what the brothers wanted more than anything else was to see each other. It had been two weeks and they had talked on the phone often, gathering strength from each other and comparing wounds and surgeries, often ending with words they didn't say aloud very much before—*love you, brother.*

Since they were in different hospitals, first they had to be feeling well enough for a trip and then they had to navigate a bit of red tape to be allowed to leave and come back, hospital regulations and all. When the day finally came, each brother set out in his wheelchair, with family members following behind as they rolled their way toward each other. Several media outlets were on hand to document the event, and both Paul and JP were overcome with emotion when they finally got to lay eyes on each other for the first time since the explosion.

"This is the first time I get to see my brother in two weeks," Paul said as Jonathan prepared to push his wheelchair while Liz, Colleen, Caitlin and others looked on. "I'm very excited... and nervous." Paul's posse surrounded him, as they navigated crosswalks and pedestrians, heading to Brigham and Women's. Liz walked beside her son, so proud of him for rallying through the difficulties of the last two weeks. They had both been asking to see each other every day and she knew how important this moment was for them. The family wasn't sure what would happen or how they would handle seeing each other for the first time, so they waited. The brothers would finally get to see each other in their new, altered state, both facing a different kind of future.

Paul remained stoic in his wheelchair as the family moved out of the hallway to make room for his brother. Soon JP appeared in a wheelchair of his own, vitals monitor still attached, with Kelly following behind. A nurse wanted to move them to a private spot, but they weren't going anywhere until they got to see each other. As JP's chair was wheeled closer to Paul's, they nodded at each other and someone said "we're taking them in here," but before that could happen JP grabbed the arm rest of Paul's chair and pulled him in for a long hug. Time stopped for them as they were finally able to reconnect after what they had been through. Liz was filled with emotions as she watched her two boys from the sidelines, giving them space.

JP quickly regained his composure and resumed the elder brother role, asking Paul how he was feeling, his face still flushed with emotion. Wiping away tears, Paul took a deep breath as they were rolled into a small reception area. Finally they were sitting side by side, looking very similar, each one's left leg was wrapped in bandages and their right stumps were covered and propped up with pillows. Soon they were comparing wounds and stealing looks at each other, facing the hard reality that their lives were changed forever. After Liz provided food for the group, familiarity set it and they began sharing easy laughs just like they were at home. Later on, Paul was wheeled back to his awaiting hospital room for one last night.

The reunion was bittersweet. Paul was finally doing better and being transferred to Spaulding Rehabilitation Center soon. He wanted to stay and be with his brother, but he knew this was for the best. "Seeing my brother and his leg for the first time made it real," Paul says. "I knew he'd lost it of course, but it was so different to actually see my older brother without the rest of his leg. It made it very real."

In total, Paul remained in the hospital for 31 days while JP was there for a total of 45. They both had issues with infections, pneumonia, and other health setbacks. JP was so grateful for the friends that insisted on coming to hang out with him when he remained behind as his brother pushed on to rehab.

"One of my buddies would come by before work and bring us both coffee to drink," JP said. "This kid didn't have to do that, but he did." And others did too. Guys came by to play cards, watch movies, and even ask JP for advice, something he is always glad to dispense. He has always been someone that people come to when they have a girlfriend situation, job issue, whatever it is. JP listens and then gives his no-nonsense view of the situation. "This is what you should do," he advises, sending them off feeling better than they did when they arrived. It feels good to help others and take his mind off himself.

The hospital staff would occasionally chastise him for having so many people around all the time. "You really need some time without all of this excitement," they'd say. "We really should limit the amount of people that come by."

JP was having none of that. "These guys are helping me get through this," he told them. "They are everything to me. My friends, Kelly, my family—I couldn't do this without them. There's no way."

He did find that it was tough to create any type of normal sleep pattern with all of the medical attention required. Fortunately a friend brought in some DVDs that he could watch. He'd play the same movies over and over, setting the timer so it would shut off once he drifted to sleep. By watching something he'd seen so often, the plot didn't keep him awake since he knew what would happen. One night he slipped the movie *Blow* into the player.

Kelly said, "Seriously, can you put on a different movie?"

"You know the routine," JP smiled, "it's either this or *Training Day*."

"This is brutal," she sighed.

Paul had his own source of motivation. He had seen his family every day and he had worked things out with Jacqui, but there was another important person in is life—his niece, Gabbie. She was a great motivator for him. "Where's Gabbie," he would ask Colleen every time he saw her. "It's gonna be her birthday soon! I need to see her."

Colleen wrestled with what to do. She wasn't sure that Gabbie should see her uncles in this condition. Would it be harmful to her or would she just be glad to know they were OK? They had tried to shield her from the news as much as possible, and thought they were doing a good job, when one day her kindergarten teacher pulled her aside. The class had been making get-well cards for JP and Paul when one of the kids asked Gabbie what had happened. "A bomb went off," she said directly. Apparently, little pitchers do have big ears.

When Colleen confronted her, Gabbie asked questions in the innocent way children often do. "Are my uncles going to die?" That's when Colleen decided maybe it was best that she see how they were doing. At first, her apprehension was accurate, Gabbie was shy and hesitant, but it didn't take long before she was comfortable seeing her uncles lying in hospital beds, looking much different than they had before.

With her birthday on April 28, she insisted on celebrating at each hospital, with both of her uncles. Paul had slipped Caitlin some money to buy an American Girl doll and JP gave her some cash for clothes shopping. Gabbie reciprocated by having a party in each room, with a separate cake for each uncle. It was a birthday she will likely never forget.

"I'm so excited my stomach is smiling," Gabbie squealed.

CHAPTER 7 – REHAB

"Hey, bud, how's it going?" the tall, affable guy said as he sauntered into the hospital room at Brigham.

JP looked up from his bed. "Who are you? Why are you here?" He was used to all kinds of people parading in and out of his room, but he usually knew why they were there. By this time he had been poked and prodded by most of the medical staff, and of course tons of friends had been dropping by daily, but this guy was a new face. Then he bent over and rolled his pant leg up to display a prosthetic leg. *Oh, wow,* JP thought, *this guy has the exact same injury as I do, amputation below the knee.*

"You'd never know, would you?" Jerry asked as he rolled his pant leg back down.

Jerry Scandiffio is a familiar sight at the hospitals in the Boston area. Working for Next Step Bionics and Prosthetics, it's his job—and his mission—to educate amputees about their options to help them deal with their injuries and move on with the next phase of their recovery. The staff at Brigham had asked Jerry to drop by because they know of his dedication and ability to relate to patients—especially young guys—trying to figure out how they will manage their own mobility and independence once out of the safe environment of the hospital.

Over 20 years ago, Jerry found himself in the exact same predicament that JP and Paul were in now—the circumstances of course were different, but the outcome the same. He was working for a construction company and was told to deliver some chainsaws to one of the job sites. While he was there, someone asked him if he could help secure a crane hook to a load of lumber. Sounded easy enough. He was used to running errands and doing anything to learn the business. Assuming that the lumber was banded together, as is standard, he hopped up on the load and in a split second he lost his balance and fell to the ground with one of the massive pieces of wood crushing his leg.

In the hospital Jerry found himself facing a decision that would affect the rest of his life. He was only a tender twenty years old and his foot would have to be at least partially amputated as his toes had begun to turn black. Part of his foot could be saved, his doctors told him, but he'd have to use a cane or crutches for the rest of his life. As he wrestled with the information, he saw a TV show with a bilateral amputee playing basketball. He had prosthetics on both legs, and he was dominating that court.

Jerry decided that he wasn't going to let a cane define his future. He told them to go ahead and remove his leg so that he could be fitted for a prosthetic that would enable to get back to the active life he loved, one without a cane. He couldn't imagine living any other way.

There were some definite challenges after the amputation that included a staph infection and a re-amputation. That was followed by some ill-fitting sockets that would hamper his ability to comfortably use a prosthetic, but he didn't give up. Soon he was being fitted for a better prosthetic, but he was still worried about how he would support himself. Construction was all he knew.

Since he had been running an errand at a union site and he was not in the union, his medical expenses were not covered. He got a total of $15,000 and that was it. Not enough to make a dent in his hospital bills, much less a new leg. He considered going to school, but that would jeopardize his workman's compensation, currently his only means of support.

As he talked about his future with the guy helping to fit him for his new leg, the prosthetist suggested that he learn how to make legs himself. He would need them for the rest of his life, maybe he could get into the business. So Jerry did exactly that. He devoted himself to studying and hands-on learning, unpaid, for over a year until he felt like he was ready for a job in the prosthetics business.

When he saw JP, and later Paul, at the hospital, he talked to them about all he had gone through. He knows firsthand what it's like to be young, energetic, and confined to a hospital bed and in the same situation. You worry about family, you worry about your active life, and especially as a laborer you really worry about how you'll make a living once you sign those hospital release papers. It's a scary predicament to be in. Jerry knows that.

"I turned that negative into a positive," Jerry told them proudly. "It's not easy, but you can do it. I know what you're going through. It's all mental for you guys. You can decide to sit on your couch and cry, or you can go on with your life. I'm here to help you when you're ready."

Paul was the first to go to rehab after being released from his 31-day hospital stay. "I had hoped JP and I could go together, but it didn't work out that way." Regardless, he was ready to learn how to deal with his new situation and become more independent. He knew that his mom and the rest of his family was there to help as they would always be, but he needed to learn how to survive.

At Spaulding Rehabilitation Hospital, he was assigned a physical therapist and an occupational therapist—each focused on helping with different life skills including balance, endurance, body strengthening, and functional activities. During his stay, Paul was assigned tasks such as balancing on a large ball while performing movements like throwing a basketball—activities he enjoyed before the accident. He would often get winded and the work was tough. Trying to compensate for a missing limb meant exerting himself in ways he was not used to, not mention he had been practically immobile for a month and was sore from still-healing injuries.

As she had promised in the emergency room—even though it didn't need to be said—Jacqui wanted to show support for her boyfriend even while she was still on the mend herself. She came to his first therapy session and returned each day to provide encouragement and just be with her soul mate. It was her goal to be there every day, but later she was put on bed rest and when Paul was released from rehab, he went straight to her house to show her that same dedication.

After two weeks at Spaulding, Paul got the good news that JP was finally being transferred there for his own rehab sessions. They were glad to be together again to be able to lean on each other and go through the demanding physical challenges together. Their brotherly rivalry helped spur them on and motivate them. Visits from Jacqui, Kelly, Liz and their family of course helped. Naturally, other marathon victims also found themselves at Spaulding. It helped to share stories and learn from each other.

They also saw Jerry as he kept in touch to see how they were doing and when they would be ready to try a prosthetic, which would naturally require training and, most of all, patience as they found the socket and leg that worked best for them. Hope was on the horizon. After weeks of tests and operations and setbacks—and of course many more ahead—the brothers were still anxious to move on with the next stage of their recovery. They were getting closer to being able to just go home.

Most of the care focused on helping them become more functional to prepare them for life on the outside. They learned how to navigate into and out of a wheelchair, how to use crutches properly, and how to deal with pain while trying to establish a new home routine. Once they graduated from those tasks, they were able to focus on strengthening their limbs in preparation for the sockets and prosthetic fittings.

Of course their support system never flagged, even though they had relocated. Visitors sometimes topped 30 a day, coming in and out to check on their pals. While it was unfortunate that they were both overcoming such devastating injuries, doing it together gave them a lot of support and comfort. "I can't even describe what it's like for us to be here together," Paul said. "We're used to seeing each other every day, so it's good to be back to that."

The guys would put that support to good use when it was time for the prosthetics. "There are so many choices depending on what you need, but the hardest part is getting properly fitted. Sometimes there's some trial and error involved in getting it just right," Jerry warned them. One of the challenges is getting the limbs ready. Having an amputation below the knee is certainly seen as being preferred because that's one less joint that has to be replicated. However, in their case, Paul's above-the-knee prosthetic had significantly fewer issues with fitting and comfort. He was able to start getting around rather quickly, learning how to walk properly and navigate challenging environments like stairs and slippery surfaces.

With JP's below-the-knee amputation, he still has significant nerve endings in his stump. That has created more challenges as he has tried different sockets to ease the pain. His doctor is hesitant to suppress those nerve endings because they are the body's natural signal in case there's a problem. Without any sensitivity, JP will have to be even more careful because he wouldn't feel the signal of pain if something happened to that leg.

"Trans-femoral amputees, those above the knee, typically have more difficulty," Jerry said. "Microprocessor knees have improved a lot over the years to ensure that the knee doesn't collapse. The toe load allows the knee to bend more naturally than the older styles did." Jerry advised that despite all of the medical advances, it's the aesthetics that most people worry about. They often get discouraged if they don't have a normal gait. Being able to walk in a group without appearing obviously different is often very important to them. It's more difficult with newer amputees because they are used to putting weight on the bottom of their feet. There's a definite learning curve.

Everyone deals with those challenges in their own way. Jerry shared his story of how he decided to go all-in when it came to appearances. "I was certainly self-conscious when summer came around and I wore shorts with my prosthetic for the first time. I felt uncomfortable, but I pushed myself. I just did it every day and soon I wasn't even thinking about it."

Then he started realizing that if people indeed were paying attention to his leg, it certainly wasn't because he looked strange. They were always impressed by how far he had come and how well he moved. Some people approached him to get advice for someone they knew and others just congratulated him. He found it was his own insecure feelings that he had to overcome. Onlookers were always effusive with their admiration of his courage.

***

Siobhan Cooper didn't give up on Paul after he left her protective comfort of the hospital room. She developed a close relationship with Liz and kept in touch with the family, following Paul's progress and providing help and input along the way. She had such admiration for Liz, Jonathan, the Norden sisters—she felt a connection with the entire family and it was exciting to see the progression in both Paul and JP as they soldiered on.

She knows that healing is much more than being released from the hospital. Not only do the guys have obvious physical changes that could affect their self-image, but serious post-traumatic stress as well. It's imperative for the family to remember that is an important part of their recovery. It's about much more than just learning to walk again. They have to basically reinvent their lives on different terms, their own terms.

It was a good sign that Paul rarely complained while in her

care. He certainly had good and bad days, but he wasn't fond of self-pity—something she unfortunately sees far too often with injuries like his. She and Paul had shared sentimental moments in the hospital, something that happens often when a patient is in such a vulnerable state and develops a strong relationship with a caregiver. He was emotional when he talked about Jacqui and he was scared more about their future together than his own well-being. Siobhan listened carefully and gave him her honest opinion, based on what she had witnessed over the past several days. Jacqui was obviously devoted to him and their relationship. That was not something he should doubt. A similar scenario played out with JP and Kelly. These couples were sticking together through this whole horrible ordeal with their family behind them.

Often Liz would come to Siobhan with questions while in the hospital and even once Paul was released. Liz trusted her opinion and found it extremely helpful to get her views on the latest medical information. Siobhan would always listen, walk Liz through the various scenarios, and provide reassurance. In the back of her mind she kept thinking about her own future. While in Hawaii for her friend's wedding, Siobhan had accepted a new position at Children's Hospital, but after the bombing, she called and told them she couldn't start right away. In fact, she wasn't sure when she could start. She had to see her patients through this first. Of course they understood.

She knew that Paul and JP would be OK in the long run as long as they remembered that staying focused requires strength. They would need to push each other to be the best versions of themselves that they can be. With the kind of support she had witnessed, they have an advantage that most do not.

***

As he watched the news about the incident at the marathon and saw the events unfold, Jerry Bowser wanted to help. He talked it over with one of his friends as he wondered what he could do to improve the lives of these young victims. Then he saw a story about two blue-collar workers from a small town. They were both injured, both lost legs, and they were brothers. Jerry decided to reach out.

He got in touch with Uncle Pete and shared his story. He's a strength conditional coach and personal trainer who was a former pro wrestler. In 2001, he weighed in at 260 pounds and was participating in a match at Madison Square Gardens. Afterwards, he instantly felt his left side go numb.

As he was confined to a bed in Mass General Hospital, they delivered the news. He'd had a stroke. He was 38. With two active teenagers, Jerry knew he couldn't accept a sedentary life. It wasn't in his nature, plus he had to cheer his kids on with their upcoming competitions. With pure determination, he decided that he was going to walk on his own, regardless of what the doctors advised. Stealthily, he started looking for opportunities when he was alone. Then he'd disconnect the wires that anchored him, grab the IV stand and head for the door, dragging his paralyzed leg. It was excruciating, but it seemed to work. Admittedly stubborn, he knew that self-motivation was probably the best method for him.

On that first trip, he made it to his goal of reaching the nurses station. He had to navigate past open doors and hallway pedestrians, and he did it. They advised him that he shouldn't be up, but he just basked in his success. He repeated that for seven days, gradually getting better and practically forcing his paralyzed side to cooperate. Finally, his doctors came in one day to check on him and he showed them what he could do. They were amazed and immediately recommended a rehab hospital, but Jerry couldn't do it that way. He would walk again on his own.

Once he was able to meet the Norden brothers, they bonded over the fact that they all lived in the same area as Jerry had grown up in Arlington, now living in the neighboring town of Medford. Initially, he'd only planned to help with fundraising. So he committed to loading down a wheelbarrow—1,000 pounds per limb lost—and pushing it the distance of the two explosion sites, a stunt he's performed around the country, to help raise much-needed funds.

However, after the success of that event, he realized he could help in another way. He and JP had formed a quick connection and JP was eager to hit the gym. "I can help you," Jerry told him. "Let's train together." He began slowly introducing JP to his style of training, focusing on the body and the mind, working from the core to the extremities. "Fitness will make great strides in your healing," he encouraged. He realized JP had the strength as he watched while he worked on chest first and then biceps. As his confidence began to build, so did his mental and physical state. Jerry knew his job as a mentor was to build the confidence so JP would want to come back.

Inevitably, surgeries would prohibit any consistent routine because each operation came with recovery time. So just as he'd get into a routine he'd have to step back for another hospital visit, but the seed was planted. Jerry told him that once he was ready and got the OK to proceed, they would get back to it and keep pushing forward. In the meantime, he would visit JP in the hospital and JP would warn him, "Just wait until I'm up again. We'll hit the gym."

Paul wasn't so eager at first because working out had never been his forte. He kept fit by playing basketball, running up and down the court several days a week. But as he saw the weight gain after being still for so long, he knew he needed to get motivated himself. Of course seeing JP do it brought out the friendly competitor in him. Jerry eagerly helped him with advice and encouragement.

"You guys are in a gym. You are making strides. We are not looking back."

CHAPTER 8 – HOME

As they slowly moved from a sedentary state to one of mobility, the brothers tried to prepare themselves for being back in the real world. Both men are responsible for their own expenses, and while it's great to have the support of so many friends and family, healing can be tough when financial matters loom on the horizon.

Being in the hospital for over a month and then in rehabilitation, not to mention the notification of future surgeries and ongoing prosthetics, both brothers realized quickly that they were without an employable skill (with roofing now out of the question), without a job, and soon could possibly be uninsured. Paul's leg alone came to almost $120,000, because he's an above-the-knee, and that is just his first one. JP has required multiple fittings to find the best option for him. These legs require continued maintenance, socket adjustments, and complete replacement in 3 to 5 years, which may mean at least another 100 grand each time. It was sobering for both brothers to realize that finances would be an increasingly important part of their overall health, they have to be quite judicious about how they manage what they have. While the future is always uncertain, they are now faced with challenges they never could have expected.

Being out of the somewhat protective confines of the hospital environment, the Nordens have been exposed to others besides their internal support system and legion of caregivers. While they are re-learning to deal with all of life's challenges—housing, money, relationships—they have quickly found out that their story of unexpected tragedy and determined recovery was being hailed as an inspiration by onlookers around the world. They are used to family and friends telling them how impressive their recoveries have been, but it is a whole different ballgame when strangers contact or approach them on the street.

Neither of the brothers grew up with dreams of fame or adulation. Far from it. At first, it was unsettling when they began getting attention several times a day, "It took some getting used to when I realized people were looking at me because of the news," Paul said. "It's humbling because that's not something that we really thought about before." Becoming accustomed to being watched and even spoken to by strangers eventually became just another part of their new lives.

Because of all of the news coverage, the constant attention placed on them, and the uniqueness of their story of two brothers—each with their right legs amputated, while just hanging out with friends for an afternoon of innocent revelry—the attention didn't wane as most current-event stories typically do. Every step of their hospitalization and rehabilitation has been documented so that people can follow along as JP and Paul experience triumphs and struggles throughout their fight to regain their health and independence. The fact that they eschew the spotlight seems to only help increase the interest. Viewers and readers watched intently as they each got prosthetics, took their first steps, returned home, and then found themselves back in the hospital for more surgeries.

It's not just their compelling story that has gained so much interest, but their positive, down-to-earth, undaunted spirit and positive attitude that has helped to motivate others. Countless people have commented on their strong will and the way they keep moving forward without looking for attention, and certainly not pity. People say it's their quiet resolve that is the most inspiring. Still, they are not overly excited about interviews and TV appearances because it was not a part of their lives before the marathon. Of course if they had the choice, they would instantly go back to their routine of being with family, going out with friends, enjoying each day, and taking their legs for granted.

That doesn't mean they aren't learning and adjusting to the attention and praise. At first it was somewhat embarrassing and they didn't know how to respond, but gradually they are learning that people are asking because they are curious and because they genuinely care.

"How do you keep such a positive outlook?"

"What was it been like to have your life totally change in a split second?"

Another reason for the connection is that so many people can relate to the brothers and their entire family. It's easy to see how these guys were innocently enjoying a sunny afternoon in their favorite city when tragedy suddenly struck and changed their lives forever. The scary and sobering truth is that everyone can relate. It could happen to anyone—it's just a matter of circumstance. While following the news about Paul and JP, everyone wonders how they would handle it if this happened to them. What would they do differently? How would they cope with it? What if their world was turned upside-down? Would they face their challenges with the same straight-forward assurance and fortitude? It's a scary scenario for anyone to consider, but thinking about the possibilities is unavoidable.

Seeing the entire family only helped add to their likeability and connection with the community. When Liz talks with a reporter, every parent (and especially mothers) can only imagine what it feels like to have your children in such a situation. It's a scenario every parents fears. Seeing her deal with the overwhelming impact of not just one but two of her sons being severely injured is moving and heart-wrenching. The unwavering stubbornness of the siblings and friends to refuse to leave the hospital rooms and willingness to take weeks off of work, putting their lives on hold to help, struck a nerve with many families as they contemplated their own situations.

From the viewers' perspective, it is easy to see that all of that unfaltering support, coupled with the mobilization of a community, only helps to inspire the brothers as they struggle for health and mobility, with dignity and strength. It was difficult for both of them to realize they were in such a vulnerable position, that they had to rely on the help of others as they recovered. And while they are simply handling it the best way they know how, they continue to unknowingly inspire others.

Since Cheryl was instrumental in helping Liz with the daily hospital decisions, Uncle Pete decided he could help on a different level. He offered to manage the influx of press requests and inquiries about how others could assist financially or in any other way to help the brothers in their recovery. Since he's retired from his job in corrections, he decided to devote his time and energy into helping to focus on the grassroots efforts to help.

One of the first media requests Pete fielded was when someone asked Liz if they could interview her at the marathon finish line just a few days after the event had taken place. Not really knowing what to expect and thinking that they should participate if they were asked, Pete and Caitlin accompanied Liz downtown. They were told it would be a private interview to get her thoughts on how her sons were doing after the tragedy.

Being the first time they had been back to the scene, it was emotionally difficult. They weren't really prepared for the makeshift memorials, boarded up windows, and groups of people taking pictures. Caitlin saw the crosses that had been erected for the ones who had lost their lives. It was eerie and sobering. While taking it all in, they had the interviewer requesting that they conduct a live interview on the street corner. Uncle Pete was adamant. There was no way that would work for them. It was too soon. They wanted to help out, but that was stepping over the line.

Pete continued handling the media and advising the family. Liz provided interviews when she could, even though she was raw and emotional, something the interviewers likely hoped for. It wasn't long before a Facebook site was established to help keep everyone informed of updates and even upcoming media appearances by Liz, Pete, and, later on, JP and Paul.

Fundraising was on everyone's mind. Questions kept coming in asking. *How can we help? Where can we donate? What can we do?*

Pete realized that he needed to become even more focused to help channel this energy and good will. As he mobilized the online presence, he began discovering rogue donation sites set up for the Nordens—but having nothing to do with them. It was almost impossible to do anything about those, the unsanctioned Twitter accounts, the random Facebook support pages. All he could do was continue building their presence and alert everyone to come there for official information.

Residents in and around Stoneham were hearing about the Nordens' progress and watching them often on local, and even national, news programs as they reached various milestones in their healthcare—being able to see each other for the first time, moving to rehab, transitioning home. Their every step was documented and filled the airwaves, newspapers, and blogs in the Boston area and beyond. Liz and the rest of the family kept fielding requests from friends, neighbors, and complete strangers.

The "Norden Brothers – Boston Marathon Survivors" Facebook page continued to quickly build followers as it was updated, often several times a day. Currently having over 14,500 followers, the page is a one-stop source that provides links to interviews, information about fund raising events, and messages from JP, Paul, and the rest of the family.

As is his nature, Peter immersed him wholeheartedly into the task. He advised both of the men that they needed to acknowledge those who were cheering them on. Of course JP and Paul were happy to do it, they just didn't have the means, especially when they were confined to a hospital room. That didn't slow Peter down. He filmed both of them from their beds, with life-saving machines beeping in the background, as they shared their thoughts with the online community. At first they were stilted and uncomfortable being filmed and photographed. Neither of them was used to so much attention. They had been content with their average small-town lives.

Paul: *Hi, I'm Paul Norden. I got hurt during the marathon last week. I just wanted to say thanks for all of the prayers and thoughts and the love. I appreciate everything. Thank you.*

JP: *I am JP—Joseph Norden, but everyone calls me JP. I just wanted to say thank you to everybody for their strong prayers and message. It really keeps me positive and wanting to keep moving forward and making things easier. It real—speaking with everyone and all the message and all the love really helps. So thank you everyone, thank you for everything.*

The recordings are basic and endearingly amateur as Uncle Peter can be heard encouraging them from behind the camera. In addition to those homemade videos, others created their own movies dedicated to the Nordens as well as countless cards, letters, and personal messages.

One of the first and most important milestones happened on May 15. Just a month after the tragedy occurred, Colleen and Caitlin Norden, Uncle Pete, Mike Jefferson, and several others walked the entire 26 miles of the Boston Marathon in a symbolic gesture to pay tribute first off to the amazing first responders who saved lives and secondly to raise money for the Nordens' future expenses. The Boston Police Force even accommodated the event by providing an escort and securing Boylston Street as the determined group neared the finish line. The entire trip took about nine hours, but it felt like there was a sense of closure. With the media documenting along the way, it showed everyone that the Nordens were a strong family, standing together through this challenging time.

It was a bold statement that Peter said communicated to everyone their message: "We're back here and we're not going anywhere." Amazingly enough, JP and Paul were able to meet them at the finish line, among the lights and cameras. Seated beside each other in their wheelchairs, limbs freshly bandaged. The brothers were overwhelmed by everyone's determination to do anything to help. At the finish line, Paul looked around cautiously before declaring, "I feel safe."

As their journey continued from one surgery to the next, the Norden brothers and their family's story kept growing far beyond the Boston city limits as they were featured in *People* magazine, *The Washington Post*, on CNN, *Good Morning America*, and countless others. They received get-well cards from around the country—even one particularly touching note from children in Texas who raised money with a lemonade stand. They got well-wishes from around the world as news traveled about this dynamic duo and their ongoing fight to walk again.

As a symbol of unity, Uncle Peter even created shirts and other items with a specially designed logo and the slogan—2 Brothers, 1 Nation. Of course there is another brother, two sisters, and countless others offering their support with the goal being to help rally everyone and keep them focused. As *they* heal, *everyone* begins to heal.

***

The small apartment the Nordens occupied in Wakefield, just outside of Stoneham, was already filled to capacity, with Paul, Jonathan, Colleen, Caitlin, and Gabbie living there, but Liz didn't mind. Having everyone close by was all she ever wanted, and being able to babysit her granddaughter was always rewarding. She loved having a small child around the house again.

But soon Paul was coming home and with the equipment he would need, space would be tight. Plus JP would be following behind soon. Colleen realized that it was probably time for her to move out to free up some much-needed room for her brothers. She and Gabbie were able to find a small place in Redding, not far away from the others. Liz naturally worried about getting the place ready. First off, they were on the second floor so that meant steps to negotiate. Also there were two floors to their house so to get to the bedrooms meant another set of stairs. As luck would have it, a company donated their services and equipment to put in a stair lift so the brothers would be able to reach the top floor.

With Paul at home, the household schedule was totally new. Everyone had to readjust to accommodate the new set of circumstances. Paul was usually either situated in the living room or in the bedroom upstairs, but traversing from one place to the other was not without its challenges.

In the beginning it was tough for Paul. "I'd wake up at night to go to the bathroom and at first I'd try to step on the floor, forgetting that my leg is gone. Once I remembered that, I'd have to use crutches. By the time I'd exerted that much energy to travel to the bathroom and back, I couldn't get to sleep again." For the first couple of weeks he felt waves of depression and anger. In rehab, he had learned that this might happen, though it was difficult to accept. His new reality was suddenly upon him, especially on those night when the house was still and sleep eluded him.

Eventually he realized that he had to cope as best he could, accentuate the positive, as they say. He had hit plenty of milestones and had lots to look forward to. First things first, he got a portable urinal to deal with the bathroom situation. It's not the most pleasant situation, but it's a solution that works. He was able to get his first prosthetic leg in late June, with his birthday on June 27. What could have been a better present than the gift of mobility? After getting fitted, he adapted to his new appendage rather quickly. He had heard stories about people having difficulty, but for some reason it seemed to come easy for him. He never really used the crutches that had been provided.

Of course that didn't mean there weren't plenty of challenges as he learned to maneuver, but just the fact that he was standing on his own was a win. The real challenge was to adapt to the new pace of his life. It's like everything was in slow motion. It took much longer to get dressed, and getting a shower was an ordeal in itself, but all of that gets better with time. Mentally, he had to learn to acknowledge it, accept it, and deal with it. Sometimes that was easier said than done.

With events like seeing the Baltimore Ravens and meeting Ray Rice on the horizon, it helped to motivate Paul to become more mobile. He knew playing on a basketball league was likely not going to happen, or if it did it would be on a much different level, but what he wanted more than anything right now was to be able to walk his dogs. Bella and Baxtor were his and Jacqui's responsibility. He hated to watch someone else do it. Liz had been taking care of them for a while, and while he was grateful, he wanted to walk them himself, not so easy when you're unsteady and trying to control two energetic Boxers.

Determined, he finally worked up the strength to begin walking them on his own. Of course plenty of family members were willing to help, but it was important for him to handle it by himself just in case he had to in the future. He needed to be sure he could do it. What was typically a 10-minute excursion turned into 45 minutes or more, but he was walking his dogs! One day when he was out with the pups, they were particularly excited. There was snow on the ground and, somehow, Paul lost his balance and ended up flat on his back. When he saw a car approaching, he acted like he was creating a snow angel to appear as if he did not need help; Bella and Baxtor ran in circles nearby. Paul was determined to do it alone.

When JP first got to rehab, he could bend his left leg about 42 degrees, and by the time he left he had reach 60, even 80 with a bit of effort, so he was definitely making some progress on that front. He had also been practicing how to navigate stairs using crutches, both ascending and descending. He now had to think about actions that were once second-nature to him.

The first day JP came home, he was beyond ready to be out of the hospital. "I had to do a press conference at Spaulding as I was leaving, and after that I got into Kelly's car and felt so alive. It was a beautiful day, and I was sitting in the passenger seat with the window down. It was awesome. I was thinking, *man, I couldn't wait for this*." Cameras followed them as they made their way out of the hospital and onto the open road.

They made a stop at Dockside, one of their favorite watering holes, for a quick drink and to hopefully restore some sense of normalcy. And then they were off to Kelly's apartment, bursting with excitement to finally be home! However, things came to a screeching halt as they both stood in front of the daunting three flights of stairs required to get to the apartment. Neither said anything at first as reality loomed before them.

JP's confidence remained unwavering. "I can do that. I've got lots of movement now." Kelly was worried, but smiled. JP pressed on. "The stairs in the back remind me of the ones I practiced on at Spaulding. Let's go up those."

Once they got around back, they both realized these were the exact opposite of the ones at Spaulding, the ones he had practiced on in anticipation of this moment. "I got to the first landing after getting up one flight of stairs, and I just broke down," JP remembered. "It was harder than I ever expected, and it was overwhelming." Kelly felt horrible, but kept encouraging him and she tried to assist as best she could. After much struggle, they finally made it up the next two flights and collapsed on the couch in the living room. The both immediately began to cry, reality washing over them like a raging river.

Finally JP said, "This is horrible. How am I ever going to do that? I hate this shit. I hate it!" Kelly wiped the tears away and tried to comfort him. It was the first time during this whole ordeal that she'd seen him exude defeat. And it was heartbreaking. There wasn't much either of them could do. The next day wasn't much better.

After a good night's rest, they both agreed that Kelly's place wasn't going to work. It was too much on JP too soon, and, frankly, it was unsafe if there was ever an emergency and they had to get out quickly. So they piled in the car and Kelly drove him to Liz's house. Paul was excited because things would be easier having JP around, but for JP it meant less independence. As the oldest he was used to being out on his own and now he was back at home feeling more vulnerable than ever before.

Liz had managed to get new recliners for both of her sons to use during their recovery. She wanted them to be comfortable. JP eased into the chair, relieved to be sitting up. *OK, this isn't so bad, he thought.* Then he tried to get up and found he couldn't. The chair didn't rise high enough for him. He needed help. He couldn't get out of the damn chair on his own. In the hospital he kept thinking *once I get home things will be much better.* It's what kept him going. But in less than 24 hours he'd found out he couldn't get to his girlfriend's apartment and he couldn't get up from a chair at his mom's house. Was this the way it would always be? Is everything going to be so damn hard? Liz was able to trade the chairs in for motorized ones that lifted all the way up, but she couldn't do anything to erase memory of helplessness that JP felt every time he sat down.

A few days later, after getting a bit more comfortable, he had picked up some tips from Paul, who had already been establishing his new home routine. But JP was still not comfortable with the bathroom situation. The choices were simple, either use a portable container, or exert the energy to make his way to the toilet. He was determined to go like everyone else, but on one occasion he had misjudged and lost his balance. JP tried to break his fall by grabbing the toilet paper holder, but that immediately snapped off the wall, sending him crashing to the floor, the sound of his left leg muscle tearing.

Kelly ran in to find him writhing in pain, his left leg tucked unnaturally beneath him. She wrapped his arm over her shoulder and helped stabilize him while he regained his balance. This was strike three. He was finding that life on the outside wasn't exactly how he had pictured it. After the pain subsided a bit, he called his doctor at the hospital, the one who had given his cell number and said to call anytime. The doctor reassured him that what had occurred was a clearing of the scar tissue. It had to happen anyway at some point in his recovery. JP and Kelly went to the doctor the next day and got checked out. The doctor suggested that JP might be ready to see a different kind of rehabilitation center and arranged a trip to the Walter Reed National Military Medical Center.

So JP, Kelly, the doctor and a couple of reporters flew in a private plane to Washington, DC and went to the facility in Bethesda, Maryland. Because of the extensive work they do with military patients, JP saw so many advances and witnessed amputees making amazing strides with advanced prosthetics. It was exactly the boost he needed after the disappointments he had faced. His only wish was that Paul had been able to come and see what their future could be like with a lot of hard work.

An important part of their recovery process was meeting their first responders. It's not necessarily an easy thing to do because, naturally, it brings back the intensity of that fateful day. At a luncheon with the Armstrong Ambulance Service in October, Paul got to meet Sean Gelinas and Matt O'Connor, the EMTs who rushed him to the hospital on marathon day. Their faces had been a blur to Paul, understandably so, and he was grateful to be able to actually talk with them and share stories from that day.

Sean couldn't believe how much better he looked. With JP, Liz, Kelly, and Caitlin in attendance, everyone got a chance to thank those crucial first responders.

In November, JP was able to reconnect with Jimma and his coworkers at an awards ceremony for the Boston Emergency Medical Services. At first hesitant, Jimma had decided to go. His wife had been following the progress of JP and Paul through Facebook and she encouraged him to attend. Typically, Jimma tries not to avoid becoming attached with his patients because it can create emotions and memories that he'd already dealt with. Regardless, he decided that the circumstances were just too remarkable and he'd break his rule this time. "You look a lot taller than I remembered," JP said upon meeting him. Jimma laughed, shook his hand, and shared stories of that unforgettable day.

The final milestone event was held at The Forum Restaurant on Boylston Street in November. Uncle Pete handled most of the arrangements for an intimate gathering where the Nordens could gather, meet, and thank the many supporters that had reached out to them during their recovery. It also meant that Paul, JP and the others were back at the scene of the explosion, the place that had altered their young lives forever. Unfortunately, Jacqui was dealing with yet another surgery and couldn't attend.

Despite some apprehension, the family came together with friends and others from the community to deal with their memories head on. It's the way the Nordens handle any adversity—by pulling together. They soon realized that it actually felt good to see the restored restaurant and visit the sidewalk where they had laid helplessly only seven months ago.

They had all come a long way. The welcoming atmosphere and generosity of The Forum—a business that had to rebuild after sustaining so much damage that day—helped to better deal with those memories. Seeing how the restaurant had come back helped to demonstrate that they can move forward. While for them it would take more than spackle, paint, and new windows, the idea was the same.

With dedication, hard work, and support, everyone that was impacted by the events on that April day has to move forward. The restoration of The Forum is a great example of what can, and must, be accomplished to prove that giving up is not an option. Some things are inevitable. There will certainly be doubt, uncertainty, and you can bet that Liz will worry enough for everyone, but that's part of the challenge.

The Nordens have to use this obstacle as inspiration. It is their responsibility to push each other to be the best versions of themselves that they can be. And the best people to do that are the ones closest—their family and their friends around the friendly town of Stoneham.

CHAPTER 9 – FUTURE

Firefighter Mike Jefferson is still amazed by how far JP and Paul have come. Because of his tour of duty in Iraq as a US Marine, Mike has friends who have lost limbs and he often shares their advice with the Nordens. "It's simple. They can have a typical life if they want it, and it's obvious that they do. Neither of them are on crutches right now. Both are walking with prosthetics, and both are going to the gym. Often one of them will come by and pick me up in his car and he drives." He's amazed that they don't complain and won't even entertain a small amount of pity. Mike hangs out with them like before, admiring their strength.

"They are tough physically and mentally. Nothing can hold them down, especially when they have each other to depend on. I still go to the bar with JP to just mess around. I helped Paul move some stuff into his house, and we all hung out over the holidays. When you see them standing in a group talking, you might not even know what happened. Paul was already wearing jeans over his prosthetic on his birthday, just over a month after the marathon. And for a minute it felt like before. Like nothing had happened.

"I still get upset, especially at gym when I'm by himself.

Sometimes I'll be running and listening to the same playlist as I did during the marathon. It's upsetting, but I'm learning to deal with it. I'll be running the marathon again. Last year it was supposes to be a mental cleansing for me, a starting-over point. Running it again will help clear my mind and hopefully make peace with everything."

Spending time with them in the hospital was well worth it, as far as he's concerned. "My job was to be very understanding, and I was willing to stay as long as necessary. We got through it together because we had each other—oh, and maybe a little whiskey here and there."

"Boston Brawler" Jerry Bowser has become a staple in the lives of the Norden brothers. His goals are to have both of them walking with minimal limp and more importantly with their heads up. "I'm going to help them get back to a life of relative normalcy. I will not fail at this mission. I will get those boys to where they should be. I know that they are not going to let a tragedy stop them."

JP called Jerry up a few months ago. "Let's meet up and get something to eat," he suggested. "Of course," Jerry answered. Arriving a little early, Jerry grabbed a table for them. Soon JP came walking in. They didn't talk about anything real important, just enjoyed the atmosphere and a good meal. Afterwards, JP thanked him for coming out and headed for the door.

"Hey," Jerry called out. JP turned around. "Don't think I didn't notice. Way to work." JP was learning that he didn't need to rely on those crutches. That's what his friends are for.

Siobhan has moved on to her new job at another Boston

hospital, but that doesn't mean she's forgotten about the Nordens—
and especially her miracle patient, Paul. She stays in touch by
attending local events and fundraisers, or just calling the family up
to see if they'd like to go out for dinner.

"They are such an inspiring family. I enjoy keeping in contact
with them. Both brothers have gone back to the operating room
repeatedly, and they are nowhere near the end of their journey.
Paul has done amazingly well. He still has things to worry about
like blood clots and infections, especially after surgeries. Each
procedure is a major operation, but he has his youth on his side
and he's strong. You never had to worry about his reserve.

"Some victims are very vocal about their survival, but I've seen
Paul be more personal and private about his experience. I've been
happy to see pictures of him laughing and smiling. That's recovery
for Paul. He's not one to be overly vocal about it, but success and
triumph for him is returning to his normal life. The trauma of that
phone call to Liz, and the fact that she pulled herself together is
still impressive to me. As a family unit they pulled together. It was
amazing to be a part of that."

As a motivator and mobilizer, Uncle Pete has continued to
help organize and channel the efforts of supporters to help, and the
Nordens to give back. He has been awestruck by his sister. "I don't
know how Liz has been able to deal with everything. She's done a
great job with that family. I love all of them and I try to be there
for them. It still breaks my heart thinking about the things they are
dealing with, but they are doing it. These regular guys were on a
corner watching friends run a marathon and then this happened."

Now out of college and working as a paralegal at a law firm in Boston, Kevin Casey still lives in Stoneham and hangs out with his cousins every week. "I've always looked up to those guys and I still do. Probably even more now. I'd do anything for them. Once JP had a surgery, so I took a Friday off work to go check on him. I thought he might want some decent food so I sent him a text. He said sure, how about bringing me a burrito. I can do that. So I went into Boston, found a restaurant near the hospital, grabbed the food and headed over. I sent him a text asking which room he was in and got this text back: *Dude, I'm in Stoneham. They let me out last night!* So I drove all the way back home to deliver that burrito."

The Norden family continues to do what they have always done—stick close together. Liz moved from the second-floor walkup to a house that's already outfitted for handicap access with a modified bathroom and a ramp at the front door, just in case. Jonathan and Caitlin live with her and Colleen and her daughter, Gabbie, have their own apartment, but of course are over every day since Liz watches her granddaughter after school. If Gabbie had her way things would be slightly different. "Why can't we get a big house with lots of bedrooms and all live together?" she wondered.

For now Colleen is working at the local supermarket and focusing on her daughter who will soon be in the first grade. It was difficult for Gabbie to understand what was going on at first. She was apprehensive when she saw her disfigured uncles, but that has subsided. "Initially, their injuries scared her," remembers Colleen, "but now she practically jumps on their stumps. Kids are very accepting once they understand what has happened." Gabbie gets to spend most days with Paul and Liz, so she gets lots of love and attention. By seeing how the family has dealt with everything, she's learning just how valuable a strong support system is.

When Paul first came home from rehab, Caitlin had to curtail her natural instinct to help him with everything. She knew Paul wanted to do things on his own. Both she and Liz had to learn not to jump up every time he or JP needed something. One of her best memories is when Liz texted a picture of Paul standing for everyone to see. She was so proud and you could tell Paul was happy. It was a time to celebrate, but also a sobering realization that their lives would never be the same.

It's all about perspective these days. Caitlin has a tendency to get involved in her own life, but seeing what her brothers go through every day helps keep things in check. One time, Paul told all of them to come to the front door and they watched as he walked inside without using the railing—his joy was unmistakable and infectious.

Now when Caitlin complains that she's not feeling well, Paul points and says, "Uh, I don't have a leg, so…" She gets the message, but other times it feels good just to forget it for a little while. When she's out with her boyfriend or going out with friends, she's able to let everything flow out of her mind and remember how things used to be. Then when she comes back home there's a constant reminder of what can happen in an instant. Not having a lot of money growing up, they all really depended on each other. Caitlin never thought they could get closer, but that's exactly what has happened. They all realize that they are each making their own sacrifices, in different but important ways, every day.

It was just before Christmas when Liz moved into her new rental, one that she thought would allow Paul and JP to maneuver around easier. Even though both have moved into their own homes, she wants to make sure there's space if they need it. Her mother had instilled the love of Christmas in her, so having both boys home made it all the more special. Getting through 2013 meant dealing with more challenges than she had ever imagined. Her family had come under attack. In a moment all of their lives had been changed forever.

Liz found in herself a strength and persistence that few knew she had. Her instincts as a mother kicked into overdrive on April 15 and they never let up. So many people generously offered their assistance every step of the way. They still do. She may not have been able to give her kids a lot of material things, but she always gave them her support. At the beginning of the year, her life was filled with spending time with her granddaughter, picking up odd jobs cleaning houses for extra money, and blowing of steam by playing darts.

Now she's filled with plenty of worry, but she knows her sons are grown men and they have their own lives to lead. They will always stay close, but she also has to give them space as they discover a new way of life. The only area where they don't agree is focusing on those accused of setting of the bombs. JP and Paul have no interest in following the developments and they won't talk about that aspect with the media. They need to channel all of their energy on their recovery. They are not willing to expend it where it will do little good.

With a little more time on her hands now, Liz is dedicated to following the story and attending the trial every day, discussing it with the media when asked and ensuring that whomever is found guilty takes responsibility. There was an assault on her family! She can't just sit by and watch. She feels a responsibility to see it through.

She's also giving back by heading up a nonprofit called "Legs for Life" that specifically focuses on helping her sons and others who suffer catastrophic injuries involving limb loss. One of the signature events of the group is the Legs for Life Relay that takes place in April. It evolved out of the walk that the family did right after the marathon. The Norden family and other participants will get sponsors and walk 26 miles as a way to raise money and honor the marathon.

Liz never imagined that she would learn so much about amputees and prosthetics. On average, an amputee will need a new prosthetic limb every five years. Between repairs, replacement parts, socket adjustments, or even entire legs, the expenses keep escalating. It's her hope that she can help raise awareness and funds that will continue to help those in need who may not have resources readily available—something Liz has experienced firsthand. "I hope we can make it easier for other people who are dealing with challenges like those we have experienced," she said.

***

Getting through the last few months has been difficult for Jacqui, but going through it with a loved one has helped them both handle the inevitable challenges. When either of them endures yet another hospital stay, they are able to help each other out during the recovery. They know what it's like and can easily relate. There's little room for self-pity when they know they need to be strong for each other. When one is having a bad day, either physically or emotionally, they know that they can help each other get through it.

A major milestone in their recovery was when Jacqui took Paul and JP to get re-certified for their driver's licenses. She had to sponsor them and take them for their tests. Paul was especially nervous because of course he was driving with a single leg, but they both passed and can now legally drive. It was just one more step on the path to an independent life. Jacqui just has to remember that they both have restrictions that they didn't have before.

"Being an above-the-knee amputee, Paul had to learn how to walk differently. He now has to swing his leg so that it will hit the ground properly in order to lock the knee so that he can balance on the prosthetic. He was able to accomplish that, but of course there are some obstacles, one being escalators. Once we were together in a mall and we came to an escalator. I went down and then turned around to say something and realized Paul was still at the top trying to time it just right. I apologized and felt bad for going ahead, but he was very nice about it. I try to pay more attention now."

Another adjustment has been the pace of their lives. Jacqui has to remember not to walk too fast and to think about what's up ahead to make sure there are no unnecessary obstacles or challenges. "I probably drive him crazy," she says, "but I constantly ask him if he's OK or if he needs help. I just want him to know I'm here, but he likes to do things on his own, of course."

Being a realtor, Jacqui is used to being a go-getter, setting up appointments, doing walkthroughs, and especially helping young people find their first house. After all that has happened, her career has been a bit more challenging. She's especially careful when she has to meet a new client. She's keenly aware of how things can change in an instant and she wants to be smart about the situations she puts herself in. She has even brought Paul along on a few appointments so he could sit in the car while she shows a house.

One of the perspective buyers actually came up to the car and said, "I recognize you from somewhere."

Paul said, "It was probably on the news, about the marathon." In that instance, things were fine, but she's still going to keep her guard up.

Every day is a reminder of what both of them have been through. "The friends and strangers who tell us we are an inspiration really means a lot. And when I watch Paul get up and face each day, it gives me strength," she says. "He's a big motivator for me when I see him handling himself with such a positive outlook. Being apart was the real challenge for both of us. Now that we are together, we might struggle, but it's so much easier because we give each other strength. He really is my inspiration. I'm not so sure I could have done it on my own."

Jacqui learned that victims who survive events like the marathon often try to control the situation because it's so chaotic. They will sometimes contemplate different scenarios thinking it wouldn't have happened under other circumstances. Sometimes she catches herself thinking *why was his leg taken and not mine?* The doctors were able to save hers and she has to accept that and move on. Dwelling on *what ifs* too much can easily bring you down.

"The situation really is what you make of it. To move forward you have to decide to put it behind you. There's so much more in the future for us that focusing on negative things is not worth it. When something negative comes up, I make a conscious effort to focus on a positive to balance it out. It could be a recent success or a compliment I got that day, anything that helps me feel good about myself. I try to take time to focus on that. There is always something better. Everyone has some kind of hardships and even though this was horrible and shouldn't have happened, it did. Coping is not always easy, but it's worth it." Not only that, she and Paul have another event to look forward to.

As far as future surgeries, she's learned how to manage the operate/recuperate cycle. Jacqui has many areas of her skin that are either still embedded with foreign matter or that are burned or marred in some way. While it's important for her to continue getting treatments and restoring herself as close as she can to where she was before, she realized the cycle was sometimes too much. Having each surgery or skin graft takes time and then she has to recover, which means she has to deal with pain and discomfort that takes her out of commission. It's a tradeoff where she is learning to balance her future procedures with her desire to move on with a daily routine of normalcy.

On December 19, after three months of careful planning involving the Nordens and the Webbs, Paul Norden proposed to Jacqui Webb in front of an ornate wedding-themed Christmas tree. It's a milestone in the young lives of many couples, and that gesture helped to build on the foundation of normalcy the two have begun to re-establish. It was a way for Paul to show her how important she is to him and how far they've come together.

After getting out of the hospital, Paul can count on one hand the number of really bad days he's had. Not to say there haven't been disappointments, but for the most part, he's able to move forward. There have been a couple of times where he just broke down emotionally because of the constant weight of the situation, but those have been rare. Establishing a workout routine has been helpful. Going to the gym with JP and Jerry Bowser is a great motivator, especially as he works to get in shape for a 2015 wedding.

When times get tough, it helps him to think about how far he has progressed over the last few months. After first coming home, there were times his mom had to help take his sock off, or help get his shower ready. Some nights he'd lay in bed and just think about how hard his life has become, but he's now better able to deal with those feelings, especially as time passes.

"At first it was weird for people to walk up to me on the street," Paul says, "but I've gotten used to it. People just walk up to me and tell me, 'I've said a prayer for you,' or 'hope you're having a good day,' or 'you're so inspiring.' It took some getting used to, that's for sure. I'm not one who likes a lot of attention, but it feels so good to know people care. I'm embarrassed to say, 'You probably saw me on the news because of the marathon,' but that's usually the truth." He admits that relying on other people more now can be tough, but it's a process and it's getting better slowing. Having to use a urinal bottle and taking longer to get dressed, those are annoyances for sure, but it's all about attitude. Despite all of the tough times that he has faced, there have been even more surprises.

He and Jacqui bought a foreclosed house in the fall of 2013 as part of their plan to keep their life on track. They got it for a great price and they knew it would be a good investment. Their plan was to work on the house slowly and eventually it would be ready for them to move into. Then they were contacted by the TV show *Flipping Boston*, and they offered to fix up the house for the young couple, complete with a Baltimore Ravens TV room and an elevator. Such kindness helped take the sting out when Paul had to get his friends to help move in furniture—where before he would have done most of it himself.

"Dealing with this and learning as much as I can is like a job right now," Paul says. "I can't take things for granted. I have to work at everything I do, but I don't let that beat me. I've learned that life's too valuable. If you're negative, things are much more difficult. Staying positive helps me enjoy the life that I probably took for granted before all of this happened."

Work and money are long-term issues that worry Paul the most. He's determined to be smart after seeing too many people end up with nothing. He can't let that happen to him and Jacqui. He and JP have talked about maybe starting a sheet metal or roofing business where they run the office and hire guys to do the work that they no longer can. Nothing's definite in that area, but he is sure that they will figure out something, and mostly likely his family will be involved in some way.

For fun, basketball was a big part of Paul's life before the accident. He was known for his court skills and he played on leagues and in tournaments practically year-round. "I'd play basketball five nights a week before, but now it wouldn't be the same. I'm not sure I want to play because it wouldn't be at the same level. That's just a fact. It's cool to mess around with it, but I wouldn't play in a league anymore." Instead he's trying out different activities like four-wheeling. It's a sport he can participate in where he's not at a disadvantage. It's a level playing field.

Setting goals has also been an important component to his recovery. When he was in the hospital, he was determined to walk by his birthday and he did. Another of his achievements was to walk his dogs. Jonathan or Mike would always go with him, but sometimes no one was around and the dogs were going crazy. He knew he had to take them out so without his prosthetic, he grabbed his crutches and did it on his own. At first he had a wheelchair and he was concerned about his relationship with Jacqui so he knew he had to walk. Being confined to the chair wasn't what he wanted, and he made it happen. "I impressed myself," he says. "I think I adapted quickly while I saw other people using canes and crutches. The prosthetic leg just worked well for me right away. The technology is so good mine is even waterproof. To be honest, I cried when I could take my first shower standing up. It was a small, but important victory."

Of course he still has surgeries in his future. His hearing is still compromised and his hand has shrapnel in it. One of the fingers on his right hand won't straighten completely so hopefully that can be rectified at some point. So it's a future filled with uncertainty.

"We've always had a lot of friends and you always hear that you learn who your friends are during adversity, so when all of this happened, I thought, *shit, we have more friends that I thought!* I almost felt like it was easier for me in the hospital because the only thing I had to deal with was getting better. My family was handling all of the stress and worry every day.

"It was funny when I get my license again and went driving for the first time. My mom was so worried. She called and said, 'Why are you doing driving by yourself?' I told her I can do it. It felt like I was a teenager all over again. I like to do things on my own, but I've also learned that as an amputee, I can't be afraid to ask for help. People want to help and anyone in my situation should understand that. I couldn't have done so much without that support. Having Jonathan and Mike J. with me at the hospital every day was amazing."

Paul, Jacqui, and JP have also been working with Uncle Pete to visit elementary schools and distribute backpacks filled with school supplies. They also talk to the kids and teach them about perseverance, patiently answering their very direct questions. Naturally the children are aware of what happened in their city that day and many of them know of people who were affected so the visits help to demonstrate that just like JP, Paul, and Jacqui, they can overcome challenges in their own lives. Being different is just a part of life. It is what you make it.

"There's no question that 2013 was the worst year of my life, but I'm still here. I bought a house, got engaged, so much good has come my way that I can't complain. I can do what anyone reading this book can do. I might be slower, but I can do it."

***

After the tragedy at the marathon, JP closed up his apartment and gave away most of his belongings. He was ready for a new chapter in his life and he knew he wouldn't need that place. Once he got out of rehab, he stayed with Liz until he was ready, then he moved into a house of his own. In fact, the same team that renovated Paul's house has offered to do the same for JP. For him it's not just a house, it's a symbol that he's regaining his independence and moving on with the life he was living before all of this happened.

He often thinks back to those long days and even longer nights in the hospital, in pain, consumed with a sense of helplessness. One night, with the water VACs on his legs, he just couldn't get comfortable. He was miserable. The nurse came in and saw that JP was in mid-tantrum. He was throwing pillows and blankets around the room.

"Are you done yet?" she asked.

"Not yet." He threw his remaining pillow.

"OK, I'll be back in a minute and we'll get this cleaned up."

JP had the same incredible experience when it came to friends and support. Like the couple of guys who would come and play cards with him and stay until midnight, even though he knew they had to go to work the next day, or the one who brought him coffee almost every morning before he went to his job.

Despite all of the support, it certainly wasn't smooth sailing. JP had a couple of real bad days where he felt overwhelmed, but he worked through that. Then he became consumed with thoughts about what his future would be like. He was used to be an active guy so that was a concern. "Will I be able to golf like before?" "Will Paul and I be able to play pickup basketball?" "What about going to the beach?" "Will I be stared at the whole time?" It was a mass of unanswered questions.

Then when he met Jerry Scandiffio and heard his story, he felt a lot better. He thought *OK, I will be able to do a lot of the things I want to do.* Like Paul with his basketball leagues, JP wanted to be realistic. Maybe hockey wouldn't be such an easy thing to do, but maybe it would. Jerry opened the door to so many possibilities that it helped to ease JP's mind a bit.

Also like his brother, the lack of a vocation or job skill that doesn't involve manual labor is worrisome. Every man wants to provide for himself and be self-sufficient so when that's in question, it can stir up insecurities, but that's something he's sure to overcome. After dealing with some of the challenges like Kelly's apartment stairs, the recliner he couldn't get up from, and falling in the men's room, he's learned a lot. A big lesson has been that inevitably there will be failures. A lot of things will be trial and error to figure out what he can and can't do.

Despite the many surgeries including taking skin from his back to stabilize his prosthetic and trying to improve his hearing, his close relationship with his doctor has made things manageable. JP regularly calls or even takes pictures and texts them to ask if something looks all right. That peace of mind allows him to focus on other aspects of his life rather than his aches and pains. "With my prosthetic, I feel like I can do most anything now. Before, I couldn't even pick something up. I couldn't carry a drink from one room to the next because of the crutches. It was tough. I was forced to use the crutches, but that inhibits your ability to do things."

Like Paul and Jacqui, JP learned quickly that it helps having someone around who is going through a similar situation. "If Paul or I find an easier a way to do something, we tell each other and compare notes. Sometimes what works for him, doesn't necessarily work for me and vice-versa. It was frustrating learning to be patient. I thought I was a patient person before, but I learned a new normal. My friend and I used to go out for coffee every day, now it's a big chore. For a while I couldn't even get into a vehicle comfortably. It seemed like everything was frustrating. I was out of my mom's house for a long time and then I had to come back because I needed help. Having to have someone around all of the time was a frustrating experience. I was so independent before this that I didn't want someone doing things for me. It was hard to get used to that.

"I tried to do everything my doctor told me to do so that I would be ready to come home. He mentally prepared me for everything very early on. One day at around 6 in the morning he came in and started talking and he finally said, 'What kind of person are you?' I asked, 'What do you mean?' He said, 'Are you a fighter?' I said, 'Yes.' He said, 'I'm here to tell you that I know your knee can be saved. We can go through a long process and it might not work, but I can tell you this, your knee is huge to you. You don't realize it now, but your knee is so important. You use 70% more energy as an above-the-knee amputee than a below-the-knee. I need to know that you're on board. If not, I'll cut your knee off tomorrow if you want. So are you with me?' I quickly said, 'Of course.'"

After that talk and for each of the many surgeries he has endured so far, the doctor was very explicit and detailed in telling JP everything that would happen. After dealing with that honesty, JP learned to trust him and any hesitation he might have had disappeared. After each surgery, the doctor was spot-on with the warning about the pain and recovery time that would be required. "I couldn't have asked for a better doctor."

JP still has plenty of upcoming surgeries. His stump has been a source of contention because of the tender nerve endings. He hasn't been able to fit a prosthetic as easily as he had hoped. There are options for a fix down the road, but his hope is that he can endure the pain and work it out. Like Paul and Jacqui, as far as he's concerned the fewer surgeries, the better. His hearing is still severely compromised with 80% gone in both ears. The fix will require that skin be removed from his hairline and put on his eardrum. For most people, the eardrum is like a circle and it can close back up on its own, but his is like a half-moon shape; it's blown out. There's not enough skin for it to close and that can lead to bacteria if it's not repaired. But he saw how miserable Paul was when he underwent a similar procedure, so he's approaching it with caution. Sometimes he gets dizzy when he lays down, but the idea of surgery is not an appealing one.

JP's needs are relatively simple. "I just want to get back to life the way it was. I want to be able to go golfing in nice weather. I want to have a good job, and most of all I want to stand up with less pain. I know these things will come, so I'm willing to be patient."

"Along the way I've learned that the tried and true clichés really do work. Wounded warriors would visit me in the hospital and they kept telling me it will get better. Every day gets better. I knew they had gone through tough times very similar to mine, but in the moment it was hard to understand how important their advice was. I wish I would have taken it to heart then because they were right. It's not an easy road at all, but it does improve.

"I listened to everything my doctor told me and never wavered from the plan we followed. I didn't do as much physical therapy as I could have, so I'd advise others to stick with it. I'm working on it more now, on my own, and in the gym with Jerry and Paul. It sounds simple, but I just take each day as it comes. Sure, I'd love to have my leg back. I'd give anything to be the way I was before, but this is the way it is. Fortunately technology is better and my buddy said I could have his leg when he dies. I checked with my doctor, but apparently leg transplants aren't there yet," JP says with a grin. "Once they get that figured out, I'm first in line."

***

After almost a year of dealing with the new realities—the new normal—for all of the Nordens and their support group, much has changed. No one will forget what they've all been through, but it won't stop them. A few may not move as fast as they once did, but in time maybe they will. That's the beauty of the future; the possibilities are endless. They have all moved forward, certainly not without challenges, but always with support. And each one deals with the aftereffects the best way they know how—and it usually involves boisterous get-togethers at Liz's house.

No matter how much time passes, no matter how many successes or failures one experiences, there will be memories that can never be wiped away. But maybe that's the way it should be. Maybe it's better to hold on to those memories, no matter how good or bad they may seem, because with time everything changes and evolves. Those memories may be the very catalyst that creates change and growth—demands it. And with time comes the innate ability to process, examine, and evolve.

There's no question that the Nordens, the people of Stoneham, and the entire Boston community face that exact challenge—figuring out how to manage those memories, process the events that took place, and move forward together. Everyone in the Nordens' circle may handle things in their own way, but they've also learned that by leveraging their small-town values and tight-knit family bond, the future doesn't seem so daunting anymore.

CHAPTER 10 – PHOTOS

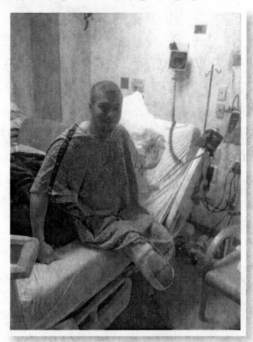

JP

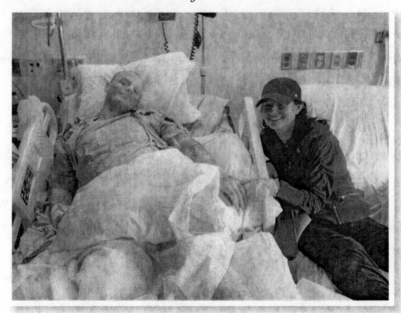

Paul & Jacqui

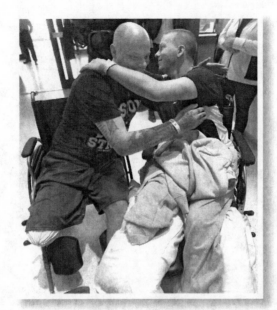

JP & Paul reunite

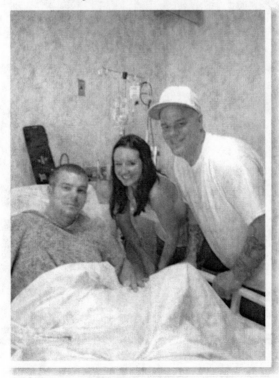

JP, Jacqui, Paul

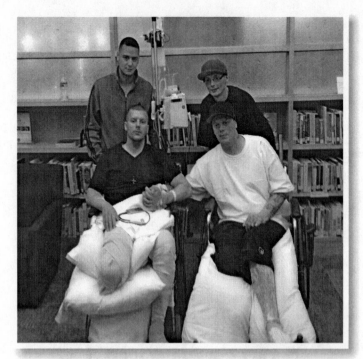

(back) Mike J, Jonathan (front) JP, Paul

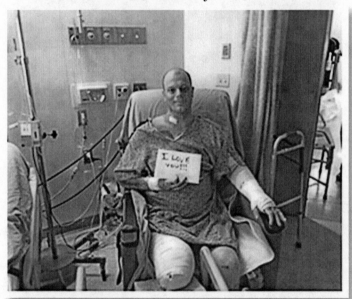

Paul's communication to Jacqui

Jerry Scandiffio, Paul, Jerry Bowser, JP

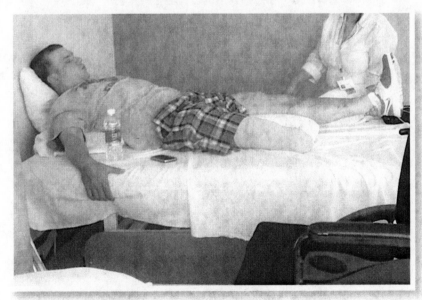

JP in Rehab

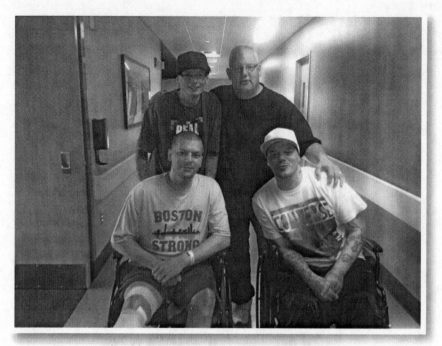

(back) Jonathan, Pete, (front) JP, Paul

Paul

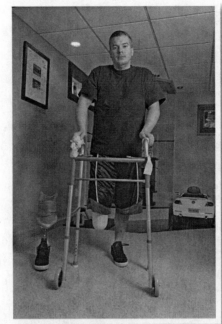

©Global Click Photography

JP

The Nordens: Caitlin, Jonathan, JP, Liz, Paul, Colleen

Liz, Paul, JP

Gabbie & Colleen

Kelly, JP, Liz, Caitlin

Jacqui & Paul

Kelly & JP

Liz, Paul, Matt O'Connor, Sean Gelinas

James "Jimma" Allen

Paul & Siobhan Cooper

JP

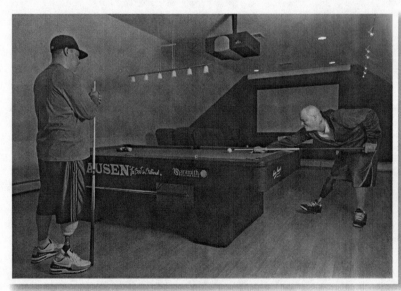

©Global Click Photography

©Global Click Photography

©Global Click Photography

©Global Click Photography

CPSIA information can be obtained at www.ICGtesting.com
Printed in the USA
LVOW13*0850300314

379513LV00004B/33/P